Ready, Aim, You're Hired!

Ready, Aim, You're Hired!

How to Job-Interview Successfully Anytime, Anywhere with Anyone

Paul Hellman

amacom
American Management Association

This book is available at a special
discount when ordered in bulk quantities.
For information, contact Special Sales Department,
AMACOM, a division of American Management Association,
135 West 50th Street, New York, NY 10020.

Illustrations by Larry Ross

Library of Congress Cataloging-in-Publication Data

Hellman, Paul.
    Ready, aim, you're hired!

    Includes index.
    1. Employment interviewing.   I. Title.
HF5549.5.I6H44   1986   650.1'4   85-26676
ISBN 0-8144-7650-3

Printing number

10 9 8 7 6 5 4 3 2 1

to **Karen**
for her loving friendship

Acknowledgments

I would like to thank all the people who guided, supported, and inspired this book in one way or another, particularly Carter Umbarger, Fred Axelberd, Geoffrey Lewis, Barbara Cerva, Paula Cronin, Wil Sheehan, Rae Andre, Dick Jandl, Dan Wakefield, Karen Oshry, Barry Oshry, Hope Spruance, Craig Esposito, Karyn Scheier, Stanley Dolberg, Susan Tulchin, Jack Warren, Sandy Rose, Joe Bierak, Paulette McCarty, and Donna Hunsaker.

There are in addition two people without whom this book would not be. Special thanks and appreciation to Carol Mann and Peter Shriver.

Contents

Foreword
An Interview with Parker Llewellyn, Director, MBA Placement Services, Harvard Business School

Publisher's Note: Parker Llewellyn manages an operation involving more than 14,000 interviews a year. So we were pleased by his reaction to *Ready, Aim, You're Hired!* and even more pleased when he agreed to let us interview *him* for this Foreword.

AMACOM: What makes job interviewing so tough?

P.L.: The toughest part of job interviewing is the unknown, and it falls squarely on the shoulders of the candidate. What will the ambience of the room be like? Who's the person I'm going to meet? What questions will he or she ask me? What are my responses going to be? And how will this person react? It's much easier to talk to a friend than to somebody you don't know. It's much easier to prepare to go home for dinner with your mother and father than to prepare to go out on a date. And I think that's the most difficult part of interviewing.

AMACOM: You must hear all kinds of stories from corporate recruiters. What's the worst interviewing mistake you ever heard about?

P.L.: That would probably be a rumor I heard about a student at a Boston-based business school who wore a Red Sox baseball cap to each interview. He felt it would be a terrific way to be remembered by each interviewer. It was—and he was not invited back for any subsequent interviews.

AMACOM: Aside from baseball caps, what else turns interviewers off?

P.L.: Meeting with people who fail to see that the job interview is truly an opportunity for an even exchange of information. I am reminded of one recruiter who described an interview at another school where a woman walked into the room and began articulating her candidacy to the interviewer. Twenty-five minutes later, at the end of the interview, she stopped talking, got up, allowed as how she was very pleased to have met the interviewer, and left. The sum total of the interview had been a monologue by the student. The interviewer was so displeased that he mentioned it to two or three placement directors at other campuses.

AMACOM: Let's talk about *Ready, Aim, You're Hired!* How did you like it?

P.L.: I liked it a greal deal. To me it covered the essentials of interviewing in a tone that would lead to a most successful interview—that is, an interview where there's a relaxed exchange of adequate and candid information.

AMACOM: What kinds of problems might this book help readers to avoid?

P.L.: The tone of the book will encourage job candidates to avoid the kind of overpreparation that can lead to a mental block and prevent them from articulating their candidacy in an open and frank way. The book is written in a style that will relax most people who are reading it, while not lulling them into a sense of complacency so they won't go through the necessary preparation for the interview.

AMACOM: To whom would you recommend this book?

P.L.: I'd recommend it to anyone who's interviewing in the job market. It's quick to read. It covers the essentials very well and in a way that I think prepares one mentally and emotionally for the unknown.

AMACOM: Thank you, Mr. Llewellyn.

Introduction:
The Worst Interview
of My Life
(Before I Knew
Better)

"We're all on the same side—we're out to get me."
Bob Schneider

I still remember the interview in all its nightmarish detail.

When the Ivy League admissions officer opened by asking how I would conduct the interview were our roles reversed, I smelled trouble.

"I'd try to establish rapport," I answered, taking shelter in the nearest cliche.

"Great," said the interviewer with a look of contempt. "Why don't you walk around the room, notice what's here and see if we can 'establish rapport.' "

I then proceeded to tour the room. Things never picked up.

My conclusion at the time was that Adolph Hitler was alive and well and working in admissions. I blamed the interviewer totally for what had been one of the more miserable hours of my life.

Looking back on this now, having been through several hundred interviews on both sides of the desk, I see clearly that the interviewer was not really to blame. True, he was strange, abrupt, and downright annoying. But so what? He could have been from outer space. It still wouldn't have mattered. What mattered was my being ready. I wasn't.

Had I been ready, I would have realized my own power and known how to act. The interviewer's opening question, for example, could have been easily turned to my advantage, or simply neutralized.

And at the very least, I could have packed a revolver.

More about this later. In the meantime, thank you, Mr. Admissions Officer, for a valuable lesson about "who's-responsible-for-what."[1] You have become a part of this book, and what was once a nauseating experience is now just a nauseating memory.

1. In addition to the admissions officer, I am also indebted here and elsewhere to Richard Bolles, whose What Color Is Your Parachute? (Berkeley, Calif.: Ten Speed Press, 1972, updated annually) has always been the classic guide to job hunting; and to Tom Jackson for his masterful and inspiring work, Guerilla Tactics In The Job Market (New York: Bantam Books, 1978).

Before the Interview

1
An Interview Is Not Like Going to the Dentist

"He had one peculiar weakness; he had faced death in many forms but he had never faced a dentist."

H. G. Wells

Right now, an interview may look *a lot* like going to the dentist. Most of us:

- Wish we didn't have to go.
- Do little to prepare except brush our teeth and worry.
- Have trouble knowing when to open our mouths and when to close them.
- Feel out of control.
- Politely suppress the urge to lunge for the door screaming, "Get me out of here."

Unfortunately, not only is this going-to-the-dentist mode of interviewing unpleasant, but it's also unproductive.

Those who get hired don't necessarily have the cleanest

teeth. Put another way, good qualifications alone aren't enough. You must also know how to interview *effectively*.

That's what this book is about.

By the end of this book, interviewing will seem less like going to the dentist and more like having lunch with a friend. Albeit, not necessarily a close friend.

2
Right Attitude, or Why Nixon Fascinates Us

"The crazy person says, 'I am Abraham Lincoln,' and the neurotic says, 'I wish I were Abraham Lincoln,' and the healthy person says, 'I am I, and you are you.' "
Frederick S. Perls[1]

"I am a Ford, not a Lincoln."
Gerald Ford

"My one regret in life is that I am not someone else."
Woody Allen

"Open your mouth," my dentist commands.

This is where my problem starts. It just doesn't seem fair that he gets to look in my mouth but I can't look in his. I feel one-down.

My dentist thinks I have a bad attitude.

"Let me put it this way," he says. "Your attitude stinks. If your teeth were as bad as your attitude, I'd resign as your dentist."

I'm working on a new attitude.

1. *Gestalt Therapy Verbatim* (New York: Bantam, 1971).

7

Four Psychological Positions

According to my dentist,[2] life offers us four main attitudes or psychological positions. It all depends on how "O.K." we view ourselves and other people.

Strangely enough, most of these positions are like being Richard Nixon for a day ("nice place to visit but I wouldn't want to live there"):

1. *I'm O.K., You're Not O.K.* This is a one-up position, or as Nixon might say, "When the President does it, that means it is not illegal."
2. *I'm Not O.K., You're O.K.* This is one-down. "I let down my friends. I let down my country. I let down our system of government."
3. *I'm Not O.K., You're Not O.K.* This is a mess. "I gave 'em a sword. And they stuck it in, and they twisted it with relish. And I guess if I had been in their position, I'd have done the same."

The fourth position is somewhat different. This one is more like being Gerald Ford.

4. *I'm O.K., You're O.K.* The motto here is forgive and forget, or as Ford might say, "Pardon me, pardon you; pardon me for pardoning you" (allegedly said to Nixon).[3]

This is right attitude.

Right Attitude

Right attitude starts by acknowledging our own worth.

In the case of a job interview, right attitude asserts:

2. My dentist got this idea from Thomas Harris, *I'm OK—You're OK* (New York: Avon Books, 1982).
3. Undocumented quote (I made it up).

1. I am a valuable and worthwhile person.
2. My experience, background, and skills make me unique, and I am a potential asset to this organization.
3. Even though it is sometimes difficult to believe #1 and #2, I will keep affirming them anyway.

About the interviewer, right attitude recognizes that he's just another person,[4] no better or worse than you.

In fact, the interviewer's position is far less desirable than first meets the eye.

Interviewing job candidates is not easy. He's got to make a rather fast assessment of a very complex subject, namely you.

Even if he's done it before, he hasn't had a lot of experience because interviewing is not the main part of his job. He probably doesn't know quite what he's doing.

He may find interviewing to be an uncomfortable experience. What if he runs out of questions or asks stupid ones?

What if he hires the wrong person? A mistake could cost the organization a lot of money. A mistake could cost the interviewer his career.

So there you have the interviewer:

Performing a very difficult task.
Lacking expertise.
Facing high-risk consequences.

And you thought that you had it tough.

Unfortunately, many interviewees tend to underestimate their own power and overestimate the interviewer's. They play the interview from the one-down position of "I'm not O.K., but you are."

This position gets triggered whenever we view ourselves as weak and helpless and the other as all-powerful. It's the way a child views his parents.

Historically, when you actually were a child this view of things made sense. After all, you were weak and helpless and completely at the mercy of the grown-ups. Your life was literally in your parents' hands. Under the circumstances, their approval was of life-and-death concern.

But things are different now.

The interviewer is not nearly as powerful as your historical parents. And although he's undoubtedly sizing you up, he's probably not thinking any of the critical thoughts that your parents, teachers, or other historical authority figures may have hit you with.

And even if he is, so what? Your life is in your own hands now. While you would prefer his approval, your survival does not depend on it.

In sum, right attitude sees the interview for what it is—a mutual exchange between two equal adults. You get to ask the interviewer questions and evaluate him and his organization just as he questions and evaluates you.

It's an inter-view.

You may be skeptical at this point. Right attitude is a lot easier said than done.

My dentist is familiar with this problem: "Changing attitudes is not as simple as changing toothpaste. It's more like orthodontia, a long and complicated process. Especially when dealing with the deep-rooted and often crooked teeth of self-image."

On the other hand, changing *behavior* is a little easier. That's why my dentist concentrates on telling me what to *do,* rather than what to *think.*

"I don't care what you think about your teeth," he says. "Just brush them."

Right attitude, then, needs to be approached indirectly through some concrete behaviors. Consider the following suggestions:

Right Attitude	*Behavior to Achieve Right Attitude*
You are a valuable and worthwhile person (or put another way, your teeth are every bit as valuable and worthwhile as the interviewer's).	Prepare an answer to the key question of any interview: "Why Should I Hire You?" Focus on your accomplishments, skills, and personality characteristics that are relevant to the position. Make it convincing.
The interviewer is just another adult with his own stresses (he probably has just as many cavities as you do).	Play the role of the interviewer and practice interviewing either yourself or a friend. This will give you some useful insights into the difficulties of being an interviewer.
The interview process is a mutual exchange of information (if he bites you, bite him back).	Establish your own objectives for the interview—what you want the interviewer to know about you and what you want to know from him. Then make sure these objectives are met.

Some Last Thoughts About Thoughts

Let's talk a moment more about thoughts, specifically your thoughts about you.

The good news is that it's always possible and highly desirable to *add* positive thoughts. In fact, a well-known and very powerful technique for changing self-image is to make affirmations, or positive statements, about yourself on a daily basis. These affirmations can either be written down or said aloud. In either case, they should be made in the present tense, even if the statement seems more like a future goal than a current reality, and be said from three different perspectives. For example, if you were Fred Flintstone, your affirmations might look like this:

1. "I, Fred Flintstone, am a valuable and worthwhile person" (as if declaring it to yourself).
2. "You, Fred Flintstone, are a valuable and worthwhile person" (as if your wife, Wilma, were talking to you).
3. "He, Fred Flintstone, is a valuable and worthwhile person" (as if Wilma were talking about you to your best friend, Barney).

Affirmations are a highly recommended way to develop your most positive inner voice.

The bad news is that it's almost impossible to *subtract* or eliminate negative thoughts. Right attitude does *not* mean that you will be free of negative thoughts, always and forever.

Suppose you have a thought called "I, Fred Flintstone, am a no-good lazy slob." There are only two mistakes you can make:

1. Believing the thought and worrying about it. Just because you have this thought does not mean you really *are* a no-good lazy slob. Of course, it doesn't mean you aren't a slob either. All it really means is that you're a person who sometimes has this thought. The thought itself is not evidence.

2. Trying to get rid of the thought. Give this approach up. It's probably impossible. You might say that thoughts have a mind of their own, and sometimes it's yours. The point is not to mind. Let your negative thoughts drift in and out of your mind, like guests drift in and out of a hotel. You can welcome them, register that they're there, and then let them be—without resistance.

3
Preparation 101: A Case Study of *Dallas*'s Ewing Oil

"Plans are nothing; planning is everything."
Dwight D. Eisenhower

"Before everything else, getting ready is the secret of success."
Henry Ford

From a philosophical point of view, the universe is a tricky place.

But as TV character J. R. Ewing might say, it divides nicely into two categories: "me" and "not-me" or in your case, "you" and "not-you."

Good preparation means knowing a few things about you and a few things about not-you. Knowing about you means being able to:

	At Best	At the Very Least
Offense	Clearly communicate why the interviewer should hire you.	Clearly communicate why the interviewer shouldn't laugh at you.
Defense	Respond to tough questions with grace and dignity.	Respond to tough questions without falling out of your chair.

14

Knowing about not-you means being able to:

	At Best	At the Very Least
Offense	Ask a few good questions of your own.	Ask a few good questions of mine.
Defense	Demonstrate some knowledge about the job, organization, and field.	Demonstrate that you are not totally out of it.

About You: Offense

"Why should I hire you?" is the key question of any interview, as mentioned earlier. In fact, it's really the only question the interviewer is asking.

Strangely enough, however, the question rarely gets put directly.

But don't be fooled.

Every important question is a variation on this theme or its negative counterpart, "Why *shouldn't* I hire you?"

Decide what you want the interviewer to know about you. What will convince him that you have the ability to do the job?

Be able to discuss your past working history, specifically, one or two accomplishments from each significant experience.

Your accomplishments, by the way, need not be anything dramatic or fancy. For an inteview with J. R. Ewing, *any* evidence of deceit, trickery, or run-of-the-mill corruption would do nicely.

So an accomplishment can be *anything* you've done, from routine job tasks to special projects, and, if appropriate, the *results* of what you've done, such as increased sales, decreased expenses, or even recognition from others—in short, just something that you feel good about, that displays your basic competence, and that has some relevance to the present position.

If you know only one thing, know the answer to the why-should-I-hire-you question.

This is offense, not defense, because it is your responsibility to make sure the answer gets communicated, regardless of whether the question is ever asked.

About You: Defense

Which questions send a cold shiver down your spine? Which ones make you nauseous?

Make up a list of at least five questions you dread being asked. Then answer them. (See Chapter 7 for some classic questions and how to handle them.)

About Not-You: Offense

Even if you are so desperate that you would marry any job, sight unseen, you definitely don't want to look that hard up.

The interviewer will expect you to have some questions. Have some.

Ideally, these questions should be real, that is, designed to do more than just impress the interviewer. The real goal is to determine whether this job or organization would be a good fit.

Write out four or five questions on an index card or in a pocket-size notebook. Bring the questions with you and don't hesitate to refer to them.

By making sure your questions become part of the agenda, you assert some control over the interaction. Remember: the interview is a mutual exchange between equal adults; you evaluate them, as they evaluate you.

Here are some possibilities, though no one will want to ask all of these.[1]

---

1. These are general evaluative questions. There are also questions designed to guide you through tricky stages of the interview, such as opening, closing, and salary negotiations, and these are discussed elsewhere in the book.

Questions About the Job

- What are the major tasks and responsibilities? What are the priorities over the next year?
- By what criteria would my performance be evaluated?
- What happened to the previous incumbent? What did he do well and what not-so-well in the position?
- How much decision-making autonomy would I have? Give me an example of the kind of decision I would need supervisory approval on versus the kind I might make independently.
- What's most difficult about this job?
- What's the growth potential of this position a few years down the road?
- Tell me about some of the main people with whom I'd be working.

Questions About the Organization[2]

- Where does this position fit in the organization? To whom does the supervisor report?
- What kind of people succeed here? Fail here? Give me a few examples.
- What is the biggest problem facing this department or organization right now?
- What are the major strengths and weaknesses of this organization?
- What's the best thing about working here? What's the worst?
- How do you see this organization changing in the next five years?

---

2. Questions Specifically About Ewing Oil:
   - What *really* happened to Jock Ewing?
   - Who's in charge of building security, and why do so many people keep getting shot?
   - What's the parking like in downtown Dallas?

About Not-You: Defense

Although not-you is not as interesting, there are at least a few things you really should know, particularly about the:

Interview
Interviewer
Job
Organization
Field

About the Interview

To begin with, make sure you know the time, date, and location of the interview. This is an area that calls for precision—not speculation. It's bad form to show up on the wrong day.

Get clear and reliable travel directions and write them out in detail.

Also have the company phone number in case you're delayed, which by the way you will NEVER, NEVER be (even by 30 seconds).

About the Interviewer

Minimal: Know the interviewer's name and position. Never tell the secretary "I'm here for a two o'clock appointment with what's-his-name."

Also know how to pronounce the interviewer's name. This can be easily checked over the phone beforehand.[3]

3. Some people are rather touchy about name mispronunciation. Consider Mr. Koch (rhymes with bloke) of Vermont. After enduring 54 years of mispronunciation, he finally decided to do something about it, and *changed* his name—to Coke-Is-It. Unperturbed by a court battle with Coca-Cola Co., Mr. Coke-Is-It vows never to go back. His alternatives in case he loses in court: "Coke-Was-It" and "Pepsi-Free" *(Newsweek,* March 25, 1985, p. 74).

Useful: Try to find a brief background summary by reviewing the *Who's Who* for your field. Additionally, if he's a business executive, check *Standard & Poor's Register, Volume 2.*

The idea is to get a tentative feel for who the interviewer is, for example, his age, interests, past work and educational affiliations, and so on.

Here's a listing on J. R. Ewing:

Current Title: President, Ewing Oil.
Residence: Southfork Ranch.
Interests: Sex, money, power.
Memberships: Oil Barons' Club.
Past Employment: Worked previously as a TV astronaut; rumored to have associated with a genie.

A lot of people stop their preparation at this point. And in fact, you *may* do quite well without any further ado. But to maximize your chances, some additional research is required.

Here's why:

INTERVIEWERS HATE INEXPERIENCE.

Inexperience looks risky and interviewers tend to be risk-averse. Ideally they'd like to hire someone who's *already* doing the job—in a marginally different organization, or someone who's *already* in the organization—in a marginally different job.

If this describes you, your preparation is more or less done. But if not, you are advised to compensate for your lack of experience with *knowledge.* Knowing something about the job/organization/field enables you to ask intelligent questions, demonstrate a genuine interest, and look like you've been around the block. Naturally you do this without coming across as a know-it-all.

Avoid showing up without any experience *or* the foggiest idea of what's going on.

This makes interviewers very nervous.

About the Job

Minimal: Find out something about the key tasks, responsibilities, and problems.[4]

This may be as easy as reviewing the recruitment ad. Consider the following ad, which could have been written by J. R. Ewing himself.

Sales Animal Wanted

A two-fisted jungle fighter to do our thing to institutional, commercial, governmental, and military accounts. BIG bucks if you can cut it, no sympathy if you don't.
If you can write, drop us a note.

This ad actually ran in the *Boston Globe* newspaper. Although short on actual job details, it reveals quite a bit about company "culture."

If the recruitment ad is vague or nonexistent, try requesting a written position description. This is a one-to-two-page formal description of the actual job duties, available from personnel departments in most medium- and large-size organizations.[5]

Call the personnel department directly, explain your situation, and ask that a written description be sent to you or read over the phone. The personnel staff may or may not comply, but in either event you have absolutely nothing to lose.

Additionally useful: Talk with someone, either face-to-face or over the phone, who's actually doing the job in a comparable organization.

Before interviewing with Ewing Oil, I'd call up Cliff Barnes, or one of the other members of the cartel, and try to arrange a brief "information interview" to explore what an oil executive actually does every day. It may look like nothing more than plotting, scheming, and conniving, but who knows.

By the way, avoid broadcasting the specific opening at

4. It's also extremely useful to get a rough idea of the position's salary range. See Chapter 9 for details on how to do this.
5. Ewing Oil may be an exception. I'm not sure it has a personnel department.

Ewing Oil. Word of mouth spreads quickly in Dallas, and no one needs extra competition.

About the Organization

Minimal: Find out the major products and services as well as the scope of operations, as indicated by sales or number of employees.

Don't rely on guesswork. Take Ewing Oil, for example. Most people *assume* that this is a multimillion-dollar corporation primarily involved in oil exploration. But there may be more here than meets the eye. Or less.[6]

To find out, check the appropriate directories for a quick thumbnail sketch. Look up Ewing Oil and other businesses in *Dun & Bradstreet's Million Dollar Directory* or *Standard & Poor's Register, Volume 1,* or in an industry-specific directory.[7]

Another good idea is to call the organization and request an annual report. These reports are often put out by nonprofits as well as businesses. Most organizations will send them out unhesitantly. Simply call the public relations office or, as a second choice, the personnel department. Annual reports from publicly traded companies are also available at libraries with a good business section.

Additionally useful: Get a sense of what's really going on, for example, major problems, financial performance and trends, market outlook for products and services, competitive position, key personalities, organizational culture, and so forth.

Do this by:

1. Reviewing recent media articles[8] about the organization. Check newspaper indexes, such as *The New York Times*

---

6. Trivial pursuit: How many people *really* work at Ewing Oil? True, the building looks large and impressive from the outside, but except for a few secretaries and a Ewing or two, there never seems to be anybody in it.

7. For Ewing Oil, try the *Standard Directory of Fictitious Oil Companies.*

8. For Ewing Oil, review *TV Guide* listings for the last several years.

Index, The Wall Street Journal Index, (Dallas Morning News?) as well as the index to periodicals in your field. For businesses check the *Business Periodicals Index* and/or *Funk and Scott Index.*

2. Reviewing Form 10-K, if it's a publicly traded company. This form is a full annual business and financial report filed with the Securities and Exchange Commission (SEC). It is substantially more complete and detailed than the annual report and can be found at most business libraries.

3. Contacting other people in the field, such as competitors, suppliers, customers, stock brokers, trade association executives, trade journal editors, and so on.

About the Field or Industry

Useful: Find out about the market outlook, trends, problems, and buzzwords.

Much of this will be revealed while researching the organization, through the same written sources and the same people in the field. Additionally, you might try skimming some recent trade journals and/or trade association publications. For businesses, also check *Standard & Poor's Industry Surveys.*

As for Ewing Oil, try hanging out at the Oil Barons' Club during lunch hour for a couple of weeks.

A Funny Thing Happened on the Way to the Library

Research sources are almost as tricky as the universe. They too, however, can be neatly divided into two categories: at-the-library and not-at-the-library.

At-the-Library

1. "Libraphobia" (fear of card catalogs, reference desks, and "general circulation") is rampant.
2. Part of the problem is that hardly anyone understands the library.
3. This is embarrassing since all of us were supposed to have learned about the library in the third grade.
4. Some of the people who stayed awake during the third grade went on to become librarians.
5. Librarians really know what's what. Or at least, what's where.
6. Librarians rarely bite, so it's relatively safe to ask one for help.

Not-at-the-Library

1. Not-at-the-library are people. Except of course for those people who happen to be librarians.
2. Some of these people are in your field and will have useful information.
3. Unfortunately, it's often hard to ask strangers for information. "Strangerphobia" is on the rise.
4. One way around this is to use a referral. "Joe sent me," you might say, even though Joe turns out to be a friend of a friend of a friend, and you wouldn't know him if you fell over him.
5. You have more Joes in your life than you think. For openers, consider all the people that went to your high school or college, even if you hated their guts at the time.[9]
6. Even without a referral, many people will be glad to help

9. For more details on how to use referrals, see Eli Djeddah, *Moving Up* (Berkeley, Calif.: Ten Speed Press, 1978), especially Chapter 8.

you. People enjoy feeling like they know something important. It partially compensates for the embarrassment of not understanding the library.

Ultimately, whether you do your research through libraries, people, or both comes down to personal style.

Some of us, according to management expert Peter Drucker, are readers, others listeners, and few are both. Put another way, some of us suffer from libraphobia, some from strangerphobia, and few from neither.

All in all, researching not-you is not-easy, but probably not as difficult as you imagine.

4
Getting Dressed and Other Last-Minute Details

"His socks compelled one's attention without losing one's respect."

Saki

Quite frankly, my attitude toward clothes probably leaves a lot to be desired. I tend to think of clothing in a practical kind of way, as something that keeps me warm or prevents me from being arrested.

However, you would never know this if you met me in an interview.

First impressions are important, and the interviewer's first impressions will be based largely on appearance. The main idea is for you to avoid attracting negative attention with loud clothing, scuffed shoes, gaudy jewelry, strong scents, bad breath, and so on.

I dress conservatively and make sure my clothes are clean, well-pressed, and appropriate. Then I stop worrying about them.[1]

1. But for those who want to worry some more, consult *Dress for Success* (New York: Warner Books, 1976) or *The Woman's Dress for Success Book* (New York: Warner Books, 1978), both by John T. Molloy.

Aside from clothing, there are a couple of other things that you might want to bring to the interview.

Run through the following basic questions before leaving the house:

> *Where am I going?* Don't forget travel directions, as well as the organization's phone number.
>
> *Why?* Bring a few notes to support *your* agenda, for example, a list of your questions and a summary of your strongest selling points. Use a pocket-size notebook or a couple of index cards.
>
> *Who are you?* Knowing the interviewer's name can go a long way.
>
> *Who am I?* Knowing your own name can go even further. Take a copy of your resume in case of sudden amnesia.

Then there are the intangibles.

Bring a high level of energy. Do this first of all by acting sensibly for at least 24 hours before the interview. Stick to your normal routines. Now is not the time to see whom you can drink or eat under the table, or whether you really need sleep at night.

If you feel lethargic as the interview draws near, try to consciously "psych yourself up." Use natural stimulants: listen to some music, move around, exercise (if you're used to it), or take an ice-cold shower. Do whatever you have to do to get your juices flowing.

Finally, bring some extra time.

Plan to arrive ten minutes early. This gives you a chance to go to the bathroom, check your appearance, and settle into the waiting area.

While waiting, do whatever feels comfortable. What you're after is a relaxed, positive frame of mind. This might call for:

- Reviewing your resume and reminding yourself of your interview objectives.
- Using some of the relaxation techniques mentioned in Chapter 5, such as taking a few slow deep breaths

(inconspicuously), scanning your body for any tension, tightening a few muscles, or visualizing success.

■ Practicing right attitude by remembering once again that you are a valuable and worthwhile person, as worthy as the interviewer, and that the interview is nothing more than a mutual exchange between two equal adults.

Or you might just want to read a magazine.

5
High Anxiety

"Anxiety is the interest paid on trouble before it is due."
Dean Inge

"Worrying helps you some. It seems as if you are doing something when you're worrying."
Lucy Maud Montgomery

My dentist has a peculiar habit. Whenever a patient looks nervous, he feels compelled to deliver his "philosophy of anxiety."

"The way I see it," he began during our last visit, "most people experience too much anxiety."

I sensed that his attack, or what he refers to as "a little drilling," was imminent.

"High anxiety," he continued, "is what Mel Brooks calls it. But I prefer HA for short."

"HA is no laughing matter," he went on, "but luckily there are several good remedies for dealing with it."

For some reason, first-degree murder sprung immediately to mind.

"With the *mental* remedies, I go after my patients' anxiety-provoking thoughts, such as 'Who is this quack and why is he pulling all my teeth out?' "

I wondered whether the jury would be sympathetic to a plea of self-defense.

28

"Sometimes, however, it's easier to work with the *physical* symptoms of anxiety. For example, rendering a patient extremely unconscious quite often does wonders for his anxiety—and mine."

That's the last thing I remember before inexplicably passing out.

A few days later my dentist sent a note:

Suggest you try some of the following anxiety remedies before our next visit. Othewise will have to render you unconscious again.

Sincerely,
Your Dentist

P.S. Before prescribing a remedy, I usually do a rough diagnosis to determine whether the patient is an optimist, pessimist, or realist. Separating the optimists from the pessimists is relatively easy. Essentially it's the old story of whether the patient sees the toothpaste tube as half-empty or half-full.

The only problem is with the third group, the realists. Realists tend to see toothpaste as a consumer rip-off and use baking soda instead.

P.P.S. In your case, none of this matters. You're a wreck. Try all six techniques.

Here are his suggestions:

Type of Patient	Physical Technique	Mental Technique
Pessimist ("I doubt if any of these techniques work; whatever you do, don't tell me not to be anxious.")	Be anxious.	Imagine the worst.
Optimist ("I feel better already.")	Relax.	Visualize success.
Realist ("Give me something practical, like baking soda.")	Exercise.	Diversify.

Physical Technique #1: Be Anxious

Sometimes anxiety is like an unfinished knock-knock joke.

> "Knock, knock."
> > "Who's there?"
>
> "Anxiety."
> > (Door slams in anxiety's face.)

Rather than slamming the door in anxiety's face, let it in. Anxiety may feel strange, but it's not a stranger. When you come right down to it, anxiety is part of you.

So stop trying to get rid of your anxiety. In fact, do the exact opposite. See if you can *exaggerate* the sensations and fully experience them.

Where is your anxiety? What does it feel like? Pay attention to the moment-by-moment sensations and try to describe them precisely. For example:

> *Vague:* "I'm a nervous wreck."
> *Better:* "There are at least a half-dozen butterflies in my stomach. I think they're monarchs."
> *Best:* "I notice a tightening in my stomach about an inch above my naval."

You might try taking this a step further by actually having a conversation with your anxiety. Play the role of your anxiety and see what words come spontaneously to mind.

What is your anxiety trying to tell you?[1]

---

1. See Fritz Perls, *Gestalt Therapy Verbatim* (New York: Bantam, 1971) p. 82, for a very helpful description of this approach. According to Perls, "Anxiety is . . . actually nothing but stage fright. If you are in the now, you have security. As soon as you jump out of the now, for instance into the future, the gap between the now and the then is filled with pent-up excitement and it's experienced as anxiety. . . ."

Mental Technique #1: Imagine the Worst

For example: The interviewer hates your guts so much that he chases you around the room with a tomahawk. You barely make it out alive. You still badly want the job but are rejected because: "Even if we never find anyone else and the company goes bankrupt, we definitely don't want you." The news of your rejection is leaked to the press and run as a front-page story in all the major newspapers. You never get another interview, not to mention job offer, in your life. All your friends, family, even casual acquaintances display utter contempt for you: "We always knew you were no good." Unemployed, destitute, and all alone you roam the streets aimlessly, a burnt-out shell of your former self. . . .

If you insist on worrying about possible bad consequences, at least do it right. Indulge yourself with catastrophic expectations. Get into it. Then ask yourself: "How bad could my interview *really* be?"

Physical Technique #2: Relax

Here are a few very effective ways to relax:

Slow, Deep Breathing

Sure you know how to breathe, but there's more to it than first meets the nose. Take a few slow, deep breaths as follows:

> Inhale through the nose—exhale through the mouth.
> Exhale completely: make sure; there may be a little more air. Exhale any air left by sounding the letter ess.
> When you feel completely empty, remain empty for a moment but not to the point of discomfort.

Then, very slowly, begin to let the air come into you.

Imagine that the air is coming in through the soles of your feet, up through your legs, calves, thighs. Let it come, slowly, smoothly in, through the sexual organs, through each vertebra of the spine, up through your neck, up to the top of your head.

Imagine this air as energy, filling your whole body. Imagine, if you like, that the air becomes luminous when it comes into your body and slowly fills it. Keep the luminous air within you for a while.

Now slowly let it flow out, not forcing it, and imagine that the air goes out carrying away with it any impurity of body or mind.[2]

2. Laura Huxley, *You Are Not the Target* (New York: Farrar, Straus, & Giroux, 1963), p. 33.

Progressive Relaxation

1. Lie on your back or sit in a chair, and with eyes closed, feel your body grow very heavy—as if you were sinking into the floor (or chair).
2. Focus your awareness on your toes. Let them relax. Feel their heaviness. Now bring your awareness over the soles of your feet to your ankles. Your feet feel pleasantly heavy and relaxed.
3. Experience this wave of relaxation slowly travelling up your legs, and so on, as you slowly focus on each part of your body (with particular attention to your neck, eyes, and jaw), until finally your entire body feels heavy and relaxed.
4. Repeat the process, if desired, this time starting with the fingers and ending at the toes.

Total Body Clench

1. Lie on your back or sit in a chair, and with eyes closed, take a slow deep breath.
2. While holding the breath for about five seconds, tighten all the muscles of your body—tense eyes, clench teeth, suck in stomach, squeeze fists, and so forth. Make sure your entire body from head to toe is tensed.
3. Then, as you exhale, let go of all the tenseness and feel your body relax.
4. Take five to ten normal breaths; each time you exhale, say the word "relax" to yourself.
5. Repeat the entire procedure one to five times.

Of course, some interviewers might look askance if you were to suddenly practice your total body clench (or any of the preceding) in the midst of a conversation.

Not to worry. There's an alternative. Choose a single muscle group that is invisible to the interviewer, such as your toes or abdomen, and squeeze your anxiety away. No one will notice this.

Does the interviewer's "Hello, how are you?" make you tense? No problem. Squeeze your toes by curling them down, hold for a few seconds, then release. Repeat as frequently as desired.

And don't worry about the interviewer. He'll never know the difference. In fact, for all you know, he might be sitting over there squeezing his own anxiety away.

Mental Technique #2: Visualize Success

Remember the bra commercial where the woman imagined herself performing a difficult task with ease, all because of her brassiere? "I dreamt I was hosting a small dinner party for the House of Representatives in my Maidenform bra" is kind of how the ad went.

The idea here is somewhat the same. Think of a time when you were feeling relaxed, confident, and generally good. Form a mental picture of yourself in the interview feeling just this way. Visualize yourself at your best, with everything going just as you'd like.

This is not just wishful thinking. The success of visualization has been scientifically documented with subjects ranging from basketball players to cancer patients.[3]

(Suggestion for men: "I dreamt I was being interviewed in my jockey shorts.")

---

3. For more on visualization, see Adelaide Bry and Marjorie Bair, *Directing the Movies of Your Mind* (New York: Harper and Row, 1978).

Physical Technique #3: Exercise

Running away from it all is often not a bad idea—especially if taken literally.

"Primitive man, to whom we trace our ancestry, was a food gatherer and hunter. He was always on the go. When he wasn't running after wild game, he and the entire tribe were walking, moving over a wide expanse of territory to find berries, nuts, roots, fruit and edible vegetation. He didn't have horses to ride until relatively recently in his development. Only his legs could take him to where the food was. . . .

We are the descendents of those primitive hunters and gatherers. Since we have the same body, we need to give it what those hunters and gatherers gave it regularly: exercise."[4]

McCamy goes on to cite a study where simple anxiety dropped 55 percent as a result of exercise alone.[5]

Put another way, anxiety is no sweat.

Mental Technique #3: Diversify

Suppose the interviewer *does* chase you around the room with a tomahawk, or for some other reason things just don't work out?

You'll feel a lot calmer, both before and after, if you have some alternatives. Prepare a concrete plan of action, including a list of other organizations to contact.

Don't put all your resumes in one mailbox.

I went to see my dentist again after practicing some of his

---

4. John McCamy, *Human Life Styling* (New York: Harper & Row, 1977), pp. 96-97.
5. The single best exercise for improving overall health, according to McCamy and others, is aerobics, for example, walking, jogging, swimming, or biking. Aerobics significantly strengthens the lungs, heart, and blood vessels in addition to acting as a natural relaxant. For further details and an easy-to-follow exercise program, consult either McCamy's book or *The New Aerobics* (New York: Bantam Books, 1970) by Kenneth Cooper.

techniques. I felt much better, although he still made me a little nervous.

"A little anxiety is nothing to worry about," he barked. "Anxiety is a lot like liver. Many people could live without it. On the other hand, a little now and then might be good for you."

I nodded my head in agreement. I figured he was probably right. After all, some anxiety is normal and useful—it's part of the excitement that comes with getting ready.

The
Interview

6
Moscow Rules: The Six Laws of Interviewing

"Tell Max I insist it's Moscow Rules."

John Le Carré[1]

Every once in a while, my dentist starts talking like a secret agent.

Take the other day, for example. All I did was ask why I needed to see him every six months.

"Moscow Rules," he answered.

"But this isn't the Kremlin. And you're not even Russian."

"Misses the point. 'Moscow Rules' means playing it by the book. Nothing more, nothing less. Old espionage expression."

"What if I were to come by every *seven* months?"

"That could be extremely dangerous to your health," he answered impatiently. "And no more questions. You know too much already."

"Sorry."

"Forget the whole thing. This conversation never took place."

Talking with my dentist can sometimes get a little strange.

1. *Smiley's People* (New York: Bantam, 1980).

39

Talking with interviewers can get a little strange too. After all, they're strangers.

Although it helps to think of an interview as "more like having lunch with a friend," in some ways it's more like having lunch with a double agent.

The same rules apply as do to a spy mission. But don't let these Moscow Rules make you nervous. It's just a matter of playing it by the book. Nothing more, nothing less.

Rule #1: Play to Win

Your life may not depend on the success of this mission; still, you should play to win.

Leave your misgivings at the door.

Unfortunately, your misgivings may not be as easy to shed as your cloak. Especially if you're not aware of wearing any.

One suggestion is to write down all the reasons you *don't* want this particular job (or work in general) as well as all the reasons you do. Write down whatever comes to mind without censoring or evaluating it.

Face it. Most of us are ambivalent about most things. The trick is to acknowledge our reservations so they don't unconsciously trip us up by sapping our energy and enthusiasm.

This job may not be your first choice. But once you accept an interview, even if in your mind it's only an exploratory gesture, go in with a high level of interest.

Don't fake your enthusiasm and don't overdo it. But play to win because:

1. A job offer will boost your morale.
2. An offer can provide leverage in negotiating with other organizations and make you look more appealing.
3. You gain a valuable contact and a possible source of leads to other jobs.

4. This organization may unexpectedly emerge as the best alternative or as a potential future employer in a year or two.

So walk into the interview as if there were no place you'd rather be—even if there might be 1000 places you'd rather be, including working undercover in Siberia.

Rule #2: Make a Positive First Impression

The idea here is to keep a low profile and avoid arousing suspicion.

First impressions count.

The best way to make a good first impression is by not making a bad one.

We've already discussed the benefits of wearing clothing. Another good idea is to say hello, especially if the interviewer seems to understand English. When you say hello, try:

Standing up straight,
Making eye contact,
Smiling, and
Shaking hands with appropriate firmness.

In general, it helps to observe the local customs.

That's the easy part.

The hard part is to avoid triggering a "You-remind-me-of Frank—I-hate-Frank—excuse-me-while-I-throw-up" reaction.

Sometimes first impressions are not so much based on *how* we act as *whom* we act like.

Unfortunately, there's no way to find out what Frank was like.

So while first impressions are important, don't worry too much about them. Your control is limited.

Rule #3: Know Your Roles

A good agent uses multiple identities in the course of an assignment. So should you. Recommended roles include:

Detective
Salesman
Defendant

Detective

Ideally, the detective role should come first. There's no point droning on about your background and qualifications before you know what the interviewer is really looking for.

As soon as possible, ask him. If the interviewer starts by asking *you* a lot of questions, calmly turn things around. "Mr. Interviewer," you might say, "before I go too deeply into my background, perhaps you could say a few words about how you see this position and what you're really looking for, so that I can keep my own remarks relevant."

Being a detective is not easy. Sometimes it takes several questions to discover what's really on the interviewer's mind. You can ask about:[2]

The Past:	"What did the previous incumbent do well and what not-so-well?"
The Present:	"What are the major problems facing the department or organization right now?"
The Future:	"What would you like to see accomplished in this position over the next year?"

You can never know too much about the interviewer's problems and needs, and the more time he spends talking about them, the better.

---

2. Although there is some overlap between these questions and the ones suggested in Chapter 3, the intent is different. The goal here is not so much to evaluate the job or organization as to find out what the interviewer is really concerned about.

Example: You are applying for the position of lion tamer. You enter the interview convinced that your strongest qualification is your rapport with lions (as described in your book *I Never Met a Lion I Didn't Like*). You quickly find out, however, that the previous incumbent also loved lions but was not a quick thinker—or for that matter, a quick runner; he died on the job last week.

You decide to downplay your rapport and emphasize your speed.

Salesman

At some point you are going to have to play your hand and make a case for your qualifications. Enter the salesman.

Ideally, you sell yourself in two ways:

1. *Indirectly.* As the interviewer talks about his problems, you subtly reveal your own experience by asking intelligent questions and/or discussing how you've handled similar situations.

   Example: When the interviewer comments on the lions' guilt feelings and insomnia since "the accident," you describe your experience with letting the lions watch *The Tonight Show:* "We found that no matter how many lion tamers they'd eaten that day, the lions always slept better after Johnny's monologue."

2. *Directly.* Here you explicitly take control of the conversation by summing up your strongest qualifications. This is particularly appropriate right after the interviewer describes what he's looking for. It also makes for a very effective close. Even if the interviewer has read your resume and already asked about your background and experience, it's still useful to pull it all together into a brief summary. Remember: the interviewer is sitting over there wondering why he should hire you. It's your responsibility to tell him.

43

Example: "Mr. Interviewer," you might say, "based on everything you've said so far, I'm confident that my qualifications are well suited for this position. You seem to be looking for someone who knows lions, understands lions, and most importantly, can outrun lions. Let me give you some brief examples of my own experience in these areas. . . ."

Defendant

Finally, as defendant you welcome the interviewer's cross-examination.

You realize that the interviewer is under the stress of having to make a high-risk hiring decision. He's bound to have some doubts about anyone, even the most perfect candidate. Far better to have these doubts aired where you can calmly address them than to let them fester underground.

Avoid becoming defensive, offensive, or paranoid.

Example: Everything's going well in your interview for lion tamer, until the interviewer notices your badly mangled left arm. "Oh that," you laugh, disarming the interviewer with your nonchalance. "One night Carson was on vacation and Joan Rivers was hosting. I've learned that the lions prefer the late night movie to Rivers."

Rule #4: Communicate Effectively

Secret agents know how to communicate effectively; they talk in code.

Everyone else talks in code as well but without realizing it.

The nearby box shows how the communication process works.

In short, the process is trickier than it looks (or sounds). But there are ways to make things easier. As a speaker, you should:

Communication Sometimes Works But Usually Doesn't

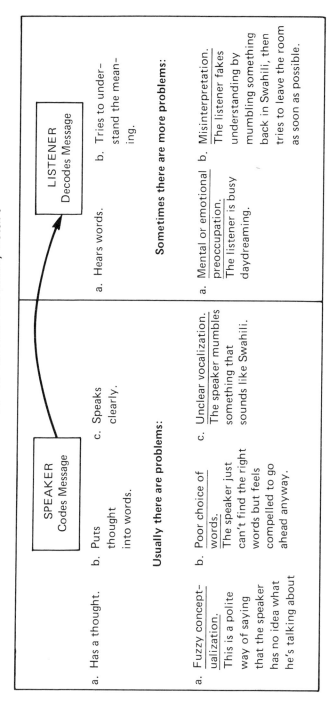

SPEAKER
Codes Message

LISTENER
Decodes Message

a. Has a thought.

b. Puts thought into words.

c. Speaks clearly.

a. Hears words.

b. Tries to understand the meaning.

Usually there are problems:

a. Fuzzy conceptualization.
   This is a polite way of saying that the speaker has no idea what he's talking about

b. Poor choice of words.
   The speaker just can't find the right words but feels compelled to go ahead anyway.

c. Unclear vocalization.
   The speaker mumbles something that sounds like Swahili.

Sometimes there are more problems:

a. Mental or emotional preoccupation.
   The listener is busy daydreaming.

b. Misinterpretation.
   The listener fakes understanding by mumbling something back in Swahili, then tries to leave the room as soon as possible.

1. Keep the message short and simple.
2. Be specific; use examples whenever possible.
3. Avoid mumbling.
4. Periodically check for interest and understanding by watching the others' nonverbal behavior and/or inviting feedback.

As a listener, you should:

1. Forget about yourself, avoid daydreaming, and concentrate on the speaker.
2. Listen to the meaning of what's being said without hanging on every word.
3. Encourage the speaker with acknowledgment responses ("Oh . . . I see . . . that's interesting.") and by asking exploratory questions. ("Could you elaborate a bit more on that last part?")
4. Demonstrate understanding by periodically summarizing the major themes. ("It sounds like things are really going well here.")

Whatever you do, never take communication for granted. Even a simple request for the time should be considered carefully. It could mean:

Could I have a *dime?*
Spy talk for "Weren't we supposed to rendezvous in Berlin last Friday?"
What time is it?

Rule #5: Respect the Interviewer

The interviewer is the wild card in the deck.
No two interviewers are alike, and therefore no two of your interviews will ever be the same.

Interviewers come in a variety of shapes, sizes, and colors. Your interviewer may be quiet and polite or loud and aggressive; he may have studied your resume or lost it; he may love interviewing or hate it. And so on.

Throw out any preconceived ideas about what the interviewer should be like.

Sitting across from you is a unique personality. Your task is not to psychologically unravel the interviewer but to gently attune yourself.

Accept and appreciate the interviewer's uniqueness.

Every once in a while, though, this may be hard to do.

Still, resist the temptation to kill him. Even agents must act with some discretion.

It's also ill-advised to violate the interviewer's space. Avoid:

Insulting his secretary.
Handling objects in his office.
Reading papers on his desk (even upside down).
Blowing smoke in his face (or smoking at all for that matter).

Common courtesy goes a long way.

Rule #6: Respect Yourself

Killing yourself is not usually called for either. So put away your cyanide tablets.

And stop torturing yourself for not performing perfectly. Perfection is an unobtainable goal, and seeking it will only make you miserable.

No matter what you do during the interview, love yourself for doing it. "You may not be able to convince yourself that you could love it all. But just decide to love it . . . And say, 'I love myself for hating this.' "[3]

3. Thaddeus Golas, *The Lazy Man's Guide to Enlightenment* (New York: Bantam Books, 1980) p. 36.

Keep telling yourself you're doing O.K., even when you don't believe it. Especially when you don't believe it.

Actually, you really have no way of knowing how things are going; it all depends on the interviewer's biases. He might have liked your initial shyness, disliked your later articulateness, and not even noticed when one of your hairs fell out of place.

So avoid judging your performance. You did the best you could. Let it go at that.

7
Under Fire:
Questions, Questions,
and More Questions

"I don't know if I answered your question, but at least I talked after you talked."

A Psychology Professor

The other night I dreamt that I was being interrogated by my dentist.

"When was the last time you brushed?" he demanded.

"Right before this dream," I replied.

"What kind of toothpaste did you use?"

"Colgate."

"Regular or new family-size?. . ."

His questions were relentless. When I finally woke up, I had a terrible taste in my mouth.

This wasn't the first time I've felt attacked by questions. Actually questions are not unlike an army.

There's even a certain organizational hierarchy about them. Some questions are higher-ups. At an interview, for example, there is the General Question, as well as several Major Questions.

General Question
"Why should I hire you?"

Major Questions
"Are you really qualified?"
"Anything terribly wrong with you?"
"What's your motivation?"
"Would you fit in?"
"Can we afford you?"

Naturally none of these ranking questions would ever risk the direct exposure of being "asked." They'd stay behind the lines and send out the troops instead.

A Major Question such as "Anything terribly wrong with you?" might send out a few tough Private Questions like "What's your biggest weakness?" or "Why do you want to leave your present job?"

Knowing about this hierarchy will help you understand what's really behind certain tough questions, especially those that seem combative or private.

How an organizational chart for this Army of Questions might look is depicted on page 51. The Do's and Don'ts table on page 52 summarizes how to deal with these typical but tough questions. Now let's have a closer look at each one.

Tell Me About Yourself
(Dialogue, Don't Dictate)

This may sound like a pleasant invitation until you realize that you could spend the next five years dictating your life story.

Where to begin? Which accomplishments and work experiences to highlight? The childhood lemonade stand? Your newspaper route?

Better ask for a clarification: "Mr. Interviewer, would you like to hear about my lemonade experience, my newspaper route, or my babysitting accomplishments?"

Better still, first find out about the job, then address yourself to the interviewer's revealed needs: "Mr. Interviewer, before I begin, do you mind if I ask you a question first about how you

Organizational Chart for a Questionable Organization

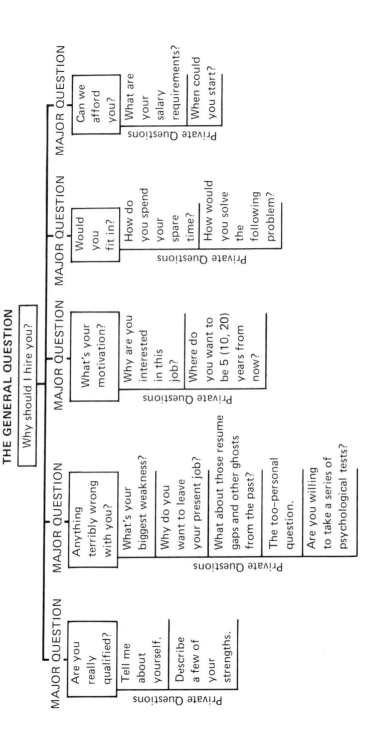

THE GENERAL QUESTION

Why should I hire you?

MAJOR QUESTION

Are you really qualified?

Tell me about yourself.

Describe a few of your strengths.

Private Questions

MAJOR QUESTION

Anything terribly wrong with you?

What's your biggest weakness?

Why do you want to leave your present job?

What about those resume gaps and other ghosts from the past?

The too-personal question.

Are you willing to take a series of psychological tests?

Private Questions

MAJOR QUESTION

What's your motivation?

Why are you interested in this job?

Where do you want to be 5 (10, 20) years from now?

Private Questions

MAJOR QUESTION

Would you fit in?

How do you spend your spare time?

How would you solve the following problem?

Private Questions

MAJOR QUESTION

Can we afford you?

What are your salary requirements?

When could you start?

Private Questions

The Do's and Don'ts for Defying
a Dozen Deathtraps
(A Digest)

What Lies Behind the Question	12 Tough Questions	Do	Don't
Are you really qualified?	1. Tell me about yourself.	Dialogue	Dictate
	2. Describe a few of your strengths.	Document	Drift
Anything terribly wrong with you?	3. What's your biggest weakness?	Deodorize	Disfigure
	4. Why do you want to leave your present job? Or why did you leave any previous jobs?	Dignify	Denounce
	5. What about those resume gaps and other ghosts from the past?	Disclose	Deceive
	6. The too-personal question.	Deflect	Disrupt
	7. Are you willing to take a series of psychological tests?	Disarm	Defend
What's your motivation?	8. Why are you interested in this job?	Dilate	Drool
	9. Where do you want to be 5 (10, 20) years from now?	Downplay	Disavow
Would you fit in?	10. How do you spend your spare time?	Dress up	Disrobe
	11. How would you solve the following problem?	Deliberate	Dash
Can we afford you?	12. What are your salary requirements and when could you start?	Delay	Derail

see this position and what you're looking for, so that I can be sure to make my own remarks relevant?"

And then make sure to keep your own remarks relevant—and brief.

Describe a Few of Your Strengths (Document, Don't Drift)

To begin with, be concrete. If you were Superman, for example, you might say: "Mr. Interviewer, I have a good high jump"; but wouldn't it be preferable to announce, "I can leap tall buildings in a single bound"?

And once again, make sure to trot out your *relevant* strengths. Maybe the interviewer isn't interested in your jumping ability at all. However, he might just fall out of his chair if he knew you could stop a powerful locomotive with your bare hands.

When describing your strengths, speak with pride but avoid exaggerated bragging. Do this by documenting your strengths with actual accomplishments. Be specific. State what you did and, if appropriate, the results. For example, it's much more convincing to anecdotally relate how you warded off an interplanetary invasion than to ramble on in vague terms about standing on the side of Truth, Justice, and the American Way.

What's Your Biggest Weakness? (Deodorize, Don't Disfigure)

Now is not the time to mention that you don't believe in arithmetic, or that your high school voted you "the strangest person we ever met."

Believe it or not, even cute idiosyncrasies like the need to bring your teddy bear to work may not be appreciated.

53

The truth is that this question can cause a lot of damage. It's a damned-if-you-do, damned-if-you-don't situation. Revealing a weakness, let alone your biggest weakness, could permanently disfigure you in the eyes of the interviewer. On the other hand, refusing to acknowledge any weaknesses may make you look defensive and closed.

The correct approach is to identify a "limitation" that is:

Job-related, not personal.
Small.
Correctable or can be compensated for.
Already known by the interviewer.

For example, suppose you were a history professor. Here are some possible replies:

Too Personal	"My sex life is a shambles and I'm constantly lusting after coeds."
Too Big	"Between you and me, I've never cared much for the nineteenth century, or the eighteenth either for that matter. My attitude's always been, what's past is past, so why dwell on it? Consequently, my knowledge of anything that happened more than two weeks ago is somewhat limited."
Not Correctable	"My doctor tells me I have less than six months to live. After that, I'll be history."
Just Right	"As you know, I've never taught Chinese history before. However, I plan to visit China this summer, and I look forward to learning more about their culture."

If the interviewer presses further for a "real" weakness, you might reply, "I'm sure I have my share of human weaknesses, but none of them are relevant to this job or would affect my performance."

As always, it's not just what you say but how you say it. If asked about weaknesses, try to stay unruffled and polite. More likely than not, your interviewer is simply using the question as a test to see whether you can take care of yourself.

Why Do You Want to Leave Your Present Job? Or Why Did You Leave Any Previous Jobs?[1] (Dignify, Don't Denounce)

"Because my boss is a moron and I hate his guts" just doesn't cut it at all.

Never say anything negative about previous employers (or for that matter any people or organizations you have ever been associated with, including yourself). Otherwise the interviewer will assume you are a negative person who at some future date will speak critically of him and his organization.

The trick is to explain your motivation for making a change in terms of moving *toward* an attractive opportunity, rather than *away* from an abominable situation.

So focus on your interest in the job or organization under discussion. Say something like "I am very excited about the kinds of challenges that this position presents (or the kinds of things your organization is doing), and I felt that I had to at least explore this opportunity."

What About Those Resume Gaps and Other Ghosts from the Past? (Disclose, Don't Deceive)

You may have spent several years wandering around the world or around your house, taking time off, wasting time, or even

1. If you've ever been fired, see the Appendix.

55

doing time. And in crafting your resume, you may have exercised poetic license and omitted mention of this particular life period— voila, le resume gap.

Unfortunately some interviewers lack a sense of poetry about this. Your interviewer may look at your resume gap the way a police interrogator regards a bad alibi.

Actually, the dilemma is not just how to explain a resume gap. What we're really talking about here is any ghost from the past you'd prefer not to discuss.

What to do when the interviewer trips over one of these ghosts?

To begin with, don't lie. There's no reason to ever *volunteer* any negative information, but if pressed with a question about a hard fact (such as Did you graduate college?), stick to the truth. Lying will only get you into trouble since many employers do a thorough background check as a matter of routine. And even if your lie is not discovered, it's bad form.

Avoid lengthy defensive explanations. Be positive, if at all possible, and at the very least try not to sound guilty or apologetic. Again, how you talk about your past may be much more important than the past itself.

With any luck, you may elicit the interviewer's secret admiration for your exploits, or at least his tolerant understanding.

The Too-Personal Question (Deflect, Don't Disrupt)

If the too-personal question were only irrelevant and nothing else, there'd be no problem. You could simply say "Mr. Interviewer, that's the most irrelevant question I've ever heard, but what do I care? If you must know my opinion about sex on other planets, here it is."

Unfortunately the too-personal question usually cuts closer to home and is in fact a trespass into your personal territory. That this question may very well be illegal, especially if it queries your religion, national origin, marital status, favorite birth-control method, and so on, is probably of little consolation. You could say "Excuse me, Mr. Interviewer, while I call the police," but this is not generally regarded as a winning play.

Here are your options, in order of increasing difficulty and risk:

1. Answer the question without any fanfare, especially if you don't feel compromised. There's no point in declining just for the sake of declining, even if the question is illegal.
2. Finesse the question. For example, if asked about plans to have children, a woman could simply reply "I have no plans right now."
3. Probe for the underlying issue. Ask in a sincere and pleasant tone "Is that a major concern?" or "Is that something that might affect the job?" The interviewer who asked about children, for example, would hopefully either say no and move on, or else state his real concern, such as limited availability for travel, in which case you would then address this issue directly.
4. Decline the question as tactfully and calmly as possible. This is always an option, so don't let yourself be intimidated. You have rights also. Realize too that a whole series of invasive probes raises serious questions about the organization's management style and the desirability of working there.

Paradoxically, there may be times when you need to *volunteer* information that the interviewer is legally forbidden to ask about—but would like to know.

Example: Consider the case of two different men being considered for company presidencies. One looked 60 but was really 48. The other looked 30 but was really 39. Both men would have seriously jeopardized their chances had they not revealed their ages.

Are You Willing to Take a Series of Psychological Tests? (Disarm, Don't Defend)

Don't take this question personally. And avoid typical replies like:

> "What tipped you off?"
> "Excuse me while I check with my psychiatrist."
> "I'd sooner die."

Tests are used by all kinds of organizations, large and small; for all kinds of positions, from salesperson to CEO; to measure all kinds of qualities, such as interpersonal skill, decision making, leadership, and intelligence.

If this question is asked, you can reasonably infer that the organization uses such tests as a matter of policy. You are not being singled out.

The two basic rules of thumb regarding tests are:[2]

1. Always agree to take the test. Refusal will raise more questions than test results ever could.
2. Be yourself and answer questions as honestly as possible.

Don't try to slant your answers to create a certain image. You'll be dead. Tests have gotten too sophisticated, and odds are your test has a built-in lie scale. Consider the following statement:

> I am never bothered by stomachaches or headaches.
> Agree ☐   Disagree ☐

---

2. Special thanks to the professional psychologists who advised on this issue, especially Dr. Paul Miller and Dr. David Javitch.

The honest answer for 99 percent of the public is Disagree. You may be tempted to answer Agree thinking this will make you look robust and healthy. It won't. What it will do is trigger a red flag about your integrity and lead the tester to conclude that you lack enough confidence to respond naturally.

In short, the best posture is openness. Avoid defending yourself either before or during the test. It will only lead to problems.

Why Are You Interested in This Job? (Dilate, Don't Drool)

Worst-case scenario: You have accidentally stumbled into the wrong office or for some other reason have little idea of the job, organization, or field under discussion. The recommended action here is to play for time: "Mr. Interviewer, I really can't answer that question until I know a little more about the job." Then ask a probing follow-up question: "What did you say the name of this company was?" After your sense of the job has focused, proceed normally.

Normal scenario: The interviewer has given you a nice opportunity to explain yourself and establish linkages between this job and any of your relevant skills, interests, and accomplishments. Communicate your enthusiasm. While you're at it, you might also mention anything that has impressed you about this particular organization.

If you're changing careers or if this job appears divergent from your past, it's especially important to provide a credible answer.

Let the interviewer know the genuine reasons behind your interest, but don't drool. This job will neither make you nor break you, and even if (you think) it will, better that the interviewer not know this.

Where Do You Want to Be 5 (10, 20) Years from Now? (Downplay, Don't Disavow)

A good answer here falls somewhere in between:

> Ruler of the Western Hemisphere.
> In this job forever.

The first answer lets the interviewer know you have drive and ambition; the second reassures him about your interest and commitment.

Sometimes it's pretty easy to figure out which one of these concerns the interviewer most. For example, if you only change jobs every ten years or during rare astrological configurations, the safe bet is to stress ambition; every ten months, stress commitment.

Mostly, however, I recommend answering concisely, truthfully, and vaguely enough to let the interviewer infer you are not ruling out a long future with his organization.

Downplay your future plans without disavowing your ambition. In other words, hedge: "Mr. Interviewer, it's always hard to predict the future, but I am very committed to a career in this field and would hope to stay here as long as I was making a useful contribution."

How Do You Spend Your Spare Time? (Dress Up, Don't Disrobe)

Let's look at some typical answers here.

1. "Watch T.V." Not recommended. Everyone does it, but no one likes to talk about it.
2. "Hole up in a cave and read mystery novels." Depends

on the job. O.K. for a solitary researcher. Not recommended for people-contact work.

3. "Exercise." Usually a good bet. It's active, healthy, and fashionable. But if the interviewer looks like he's about to keel over any minute from cardiovascular disease, don't harp on it.

4. "Run a small city in Maine as a hobby." Could be touchy. Might give the impression that outside time demands will conflict with the job.

5. "Take strange drugs, join religious cults, and watch *The Rocky Horror Picture Show* over and over." No good. Ask yourself "Would Ronald Reagan approve of this?" If not, avoid mentioning.

6. "Sky-dive." Only works if you really do. Don't get carried away trying to appear "interesting." Being down-to-earth is just fine.

7. "Sit around with the family and drink a lot of milk." Not bad. Looks normal and real, which is basically what you're after.

In short, mention a few of the ways you actually do use your time, with discretion.

How Would You Solve the Following Problem? (Deliberate, Don't Dash)

"Suppose you were the President of the United States. What would you do about the budget deficit?"

Your first reaction to a question like this might range from "Damned if I know" to "What's a budget deficit?"[3]

Surprisingly, if you put a little polish on these first reactions, you can end up with a pretty good answer.

3. In retrospect, either of these answers would have been better than the one Mondale gave in 1984 ("Raise taxes").

There's probably a good reason why you find yourself without an answer. The problem may be too complicated to yield an immediate solution; it may be beyond your expertise; or there may not even be an answer.

Better to deliberate than dash in with a quick fix. The quick fix runs the risk of making you look superficial and may even insult the interviewer—who may have been struggling with this problem for some time.

Begin by making sure you understand the dimensions of the problem. Ask a few clarifying questions, such as "Am I a Democrat or a Republican?" or "When am I up for re-election?"

If after a few such questions, the problem still defies solution, then ask for time. "Mr. Interviewer," you might say, "I'm sure I can come up with some suggestions, but I'd like a while to think about your problem. Let me get back to you in a couple of years."

If you doubt that even time would help, your answer is easy: "I don't know. Excuse me for a moment while I call a few leading economists."

This can be refreshingly positive since it shows you to be a person who knows his limitations and is unafraid to admit them—far preferable to the person who pretends to know everything.

The moral here is simple. Don't be afraid of your (apparent) limitations; they may even turn out to be strengths.

What Are Your Salary Requirements and When Could You Start? (Delay, Don't Derail)

Don't be tempted by these questions. You might say "I won't accept anything less than $20,900 because that's what my brother-in-law Harold makes" or "I can start anytime after the next full moon."

But unless you are very close to an actual job offer, now is not the time to dicker. Getting into specifics early on about time and money can only hurt you because:

- Agreement on these "superficial" points won't get you the job.
- Disagreement, on the other hand, could eliminate you.
- At the very least, you'll end up with a lot less than if you had waited till the interviewer was psychologically hooked on hiring you and hence willing to offer a sweeter package.

If pressed early on about salary or time requirements, answer "I'm open and negotiable" or "I'm sure that wouldn't be a problem once we reached an agreement about the position."

Don't let yourself get derailed into premature negotiations when your negotiating position is weak. "Money talks, nobody walks" may be true sometimes, but in this case I'd recommend that if money talks, you run for the hills.

Well, that about covers it.

Don't despair. It's totally unnecessary to memorize any of the answers in this chapter. Just remember that you have more choices than first meet the eye. Flexibility is the key. You can:

Answer the question as is.
Ask for a clarification.
Think about the question for a few seconds—or a few days.
Ask a counter-question first.
Answer elusively.
Say "I don't know."
Decline to answer entirely.

Deploy your options. Don't delude yourself that you have none.

8
A Peek at Nonverbal Communication

"Here's looking at you, kid."
Humphrey Bogart (in *Casablanca*)

"You can observe a lot just by watching."
Yogi Berra

When was the last time you thought about gravity? Lucky for you, gravity continues to do its job whether you're grateful or not. Perhaps it consoles itself by thinking "Just because no one ever sends me a postcard, doesn't mean I don't exist."

Nonverbal communication is a similar kind of thing. We may not think about it much, but it's there.

Nonverbal communication can be anything from punching the interviewer in the nose to sending him flowers. Usually, however, we're talking about such things as:

Voice (tone, speed, volume)
Facial expressions
Eye contact
Gestures
Body posture

Believe it or not, our impressions of other people are mostly based on their nonverbal behavior.

As the saying goes, it's not *what* you say (that is, the words) but *how* you say it (that is, the nonverbal communication).

Consider the word hello. This single word can mean very different things depending on the tone of voice:

Hello: Nice to meet you.
Hellooo?: Is anybody home?
Hello!:   It's great to see you.
Hello!!!:   Take off all your clothes immediately.
hello: Drop dead.

You should know enough about your own nonverbal behavior to make sure it's not disruptive.

Let's look at eye contact, for example. As with most nonverbal behavior, the goal is moderation.

Some people misinterpret good eye contact to mean continuous eye contact. But this is usually neither comfortable nor natural.

The typical pattern is to look at the interviewer when he's speaking, less often when you're speaking. Periodic eye contact is important, but there's no reason to overdo it.

Avoid extreme behavior like never looking at the interviewer at all or never looking away; then do what feels natural.

The same thing applies to other body language. Role-play an interview and invite feedback on your nonverbal behavior.

Ask your partner to focus his feedback on any behavior that was particularly distracting. For example you may:

Talk too loud/soft/fast/slow.
Move too much/too little.
Sit too slouchy/too stiffly.
Shake hands too limply/too bone-crushingly.

You may be completely unaware of some of your behaviors or of their effect on others.

Of course, getting feedback on your nonverbal style does have some limitations.

For one thing, not everyone will read your behavior the same way.

Covering your mouth with your hand, for example, may be seen as:

Defensive and closed.
Fearful of exposing bad breath.
About to throw up.

Realize also that there's a limit to how much of your nonverbal behavior you may want to be aware of or change. Basically what we're after here is some fine-tuning, not a major personality transformation.

Within these parameters, some feedback is useful.

Don't forget about the interviewer's nonverbal behavior as well. When you speak, does he:

Stare off vacantly into space?
Look at his watch?
Move restlessly?
Snore?

If so, it's probably time to do something different to re-engage his attention. Cut your remarks short and switch the focus to him, his problems, and his unanswered questions about you.

For example: "Mr. Interviewer, I couldn't help noticing that you've fallen asleep. Before you doze off again, let me ask you a quick question. How much would you sell me that tie for?"

There are two main dangers associated with nonverbal communication:

1. Not thinking about it enough.
2. Thinking about it too much.

It's a lot like table manners—a little knowledge goes a long way. Knowing something about knives and forks can often prove quite helpful. On the other hand, if the meal is only about silverware, everyone goes away hungry.

So take a peek at nonverbal behavior (both yours and the interviewer's) from time to time. But don't stare.

9
Money Talk

"We're overpaying him, but he's worth it."
Samuel Goldwyn

I tried to hire a fishwife to ghostwrite this chapter, but we couldn't come to terms. As I was leaving, she screamed out some free advice:

"Tell them to haggle!"
"Everything's negotiable."
"This week's special is scrod."

The fishwife was essentially right; most salaries are negotiable. To appreciate this, you must understand two facts:

Fact One: Most employers tend to think in terms of salary ranges, and there is usually ample room to maneuver within a given range.
Fact Two: Sometimes the range itself can be finessed.

Allow me to elaborate.

Fact One: Employers Tend to Think in Terms of Salary Ranges

"Give him fifteen to twenty" could either be a jail sentence or a compensation offer.

Some things just naturally come in ranges. In the case of job offers and prison terms, the range provides built-in wiggle room to respond to developments over time.

A salary range, for example, allows for increased compensation to match growth in job experience and proficiency.

The key point about salary ranges is that you can theoretically start *anywhere* within the range. There's no rule that says you have to start at the minimum point.

Negotiating a starting salary is much like trying to get a lenient prison sentence.

"I am not your ordinary widget-maker (criminal)," the job applicant (defendant) argues. "Take a good look at my background (clean record) and consider my potential contribution to this organization (society). . . ."

The idea is to make the strongest case possible for your experience, education, and skills—and know something about negotiating.

Fact Two: Sometimes the Range Itself Can Be Finessed

Salary ranges don't just get plucked out of thin air. Usually they're embedded in an organizational salary structure. Organizations create these structures to achieve:

> *External Balance:* Also known as "Let's not look stupid in the eyes of the world," external balance means figuring out what similar organizations pay for similar positions and then paying the going rate.
>
> *Internal Balance:* Also known as "I don't want every Tom, Dick, and Harry who works here trying to slit my throat," internal balance means paying people equitably in relation to each other, by analyzing and rating their tasks and responsibilities.

In short, salary ranges depend on making inter- and intra-organizational comparisons, based on the position's tasks and responsibilities.

The best way to finesse a range is to:

- Apply for unique, one-of-a-kind positions where comparisons are difficult to make and the range is more fluid to begin with; or
- Renegotiate the position's tasks and responsibilities so that the job is enlarged and redefined, warranting a new salary range.

Granted, this is not easy.

Let's sum up this business about salaries being negotiable with an example. You are applying for a position as security guard at the local bank, and you do the following:

1. You fight your way up the range by pointing with pride to your previous ten years experience as an ex-con and to your unique insights into the criminal mind.
2. You also try to finesse the range by enlarging the position. In addition to performing the routine security functions, you propose to design and star in a series of television ads, to be known as the "We dare you to rob us" campaign.
3. Failing all else, you casually refer to the bank president as Dad.

Your goal in these negotiations, by the way, is to get as much money as possible.

There are sound reasons for playing for a maximum figure:

1. The easiest time to get a raise is NOW; your negotiating position will probably never be stronger.
2. Your starting salary will definitely affect future compensation with this organization, and perhaps with other

employers as well; they may be influenced by your previous earnings.

and even if you're totally disinterested in money:

3. Pay = level of responsibility = organizational power, status, respect, and so forth.
4. You communicate that you place a high value on your worth.

So try not to feel guilty or apologetic about negotiating.

Hopefully, by now you're convinced that most salaries are negotiable and that you have a right to haggle.

Let's see how to negotiate most effectively, by considering a step-by-step approach:

Step One:	Know your reservation price.
Step Two:	Estimate their reservation price.
Step Three:	Consider the zone of agreement.
Step Four:	Watch your timing.
Step Five:	Let them make the first bid.
Step Six:	Go 20 percent over their offer.
Step Seven:	Check out the entire package
Step Eight:	Sleep on it.

Don't worry. It's not that complicated.

Step One: Know Your Reservation Price

Your reservation price is the *minimum* salary you would accept and can be based on any number of criteria:

Your budgetary needs.
Your perceived market worth.
What the next-door neighbor is getting.

Often one's current salary is a factor. For example, you might refuse to accept a cut in pay (reservation price = current salary). Or, as some career consultants advise, you might refuse to change jobs unless there is a 20 percent pay increase.

Then again, pay may be less important than other variables, such as location, and you may even be willing to take a cut in pay.

How you determine your reservation price is your own business. The important thing is to be clear in advance. Knowing your nonnegotiable, rock-bottom figure will give you an anchor during negotiations and will prevent you from being bargained down too low.

Step Two: Estimate Their Reservation Price

This is the *maximum* salary you think they would offer, based on your sense of the position's salary range.

Remember, this salary range was partly determined by external information, and this information is available to you too. Contact people who are active or knowledgeable about the field, such as two or three of the following:

- Your counterpart in a comparable organization. Avoid asking this person what their actual salary is; ask what they think the range would be in their company for someone with your qualifications.
- Personnel department in a comparable organization. Ask for someone in wage and salary administration.
- Trade association executive. Check the Yellow Pages for a listing of local associations; these associations often conduct salary surveys.
- Trade journal editor. Ask anyone in the field for the name of relevant journals; these journals often publish surveys.

ployment agencies. Ask for someone knowledgeable
about your specific field.
Executive recruiters. Ask for someone knowledgeable
about your specific field.
- College placement officers. Try the largest and best-
known local universities, even if you didn't go there.

This research can easily be done by phone in less than an hour,
and it's well worth it.

Step Three: Consider the Zone of Agreement

This zone includes all settlements that accommodate both your
reservation price and theirs.
Example #1: Your reservation price is $20,000. Employer's
reservation price is $25,000. Hence, any salary that is greater
than $20,000 but less than $25,000 would be potentially ac-
ceptable to both parties.
Unfortunately, it's not always that simple.
Example #2: Your reservation price is $20,000. Employer's
reservation price is $15,000. There is no zone of agreement and
negotiations will break down.
Example #3: Your reservation price is $20,000. Employer's
reservation price is $20,500. The zone of agreement is very
narrow and may be difficult to locate.
In sum, the zone of agreement can be broad, narrow, or
nonexistent. Negotiations will look different in each case.

Step Four: Watch Your Timing

Timing is everything. The best time to talk money is somewhere
in between "We must have you" and "We got you," as the

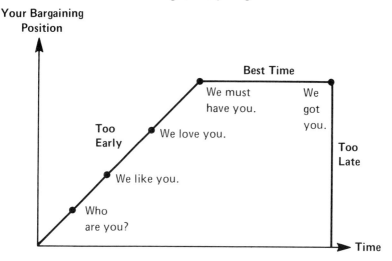

above illustration shows. Basically, the longer you delay salary negotiations, the better—up to a point.

Once the organization is hooked on hiring you, they won't want to even think about their second choice, regardless of any price differential. Until you get to that point, stall.[1]

INTERVIEWER: "What are your salary requirements?"
YOU: "I'm open and negotiable."

If pressed further, add:

> "I need to hear more about the position."
>
> or
>
> "I'm sure that should we come to an agreement about the position, we'll be able to work out the salary."

Your goal is to gently move the interviewer off the subject,

1. I am indebted here and elsewhere in this chapter to the work of Dr. Frederick Axelberd.

while at the same time providing reassurance that agreement on salary will not be a problem.

As always, a calm, positive manner goes a long way.

Let me reassure you about the legitimacy of stalling. You are communicating to the interviewer that you don't just have a single price tag on your head but that your salary requirements might vary (maybe they would, maybe they wouldn't) on the basis of any number of factors such as:

1. Tasks and responsibilities.
2. Working conditions.
3. Opportunities for growth and advancement.

Suppose I earned a living by cleaning other people's houses. "How much do you charge?" they might ask. My answer would be "It depends." And in all truth it probably would be influenced by some of the following considerations:

1. Do I have to clean the toilet? (What exactly are the tasks and responsibilities?)
2. Are there any rabid dogs around? (What are the working conditions?)
3. Is the butler about to retire? (Are there opportunities for growth and advancement?)

I'd be a fool to jump in with a set price before considering exactly what I was getting into.

In short, it's quite reasonable to *fully* explore both the position and the organization before broaching the subject of salary.

Several interviews may go by without any talk of money at all, and this is fine.

There comes a time, however, when your bargaining position is strongest. This is *after* the employer is psychologically hooked but *before* you have accepted the job. Now is the time to talk money.

Step Five: Let Them Make the First Bid

You do this either by raising the subject yourself (for example, "What is your compensation plan?") or by parrying one of their questions.

INTERVIEWER:	"What are your salary requirements?"
YOU:	"I'm open and negotiable. What would be a starting salary here for someone with my qualifications?"

By this point, of course, you are a master at the "flexible" answer. Here's the plan:

1. Interviewer makes the opening bid. This figure is not his reservation price but gives you one more clue about it.
2. You make a counterbid, above his opening bid *and* above your updated estimate of his reservation price.
3. Settlement is higher than the interviewer's opening bid, lower than your counterbid, and hopefully very near the interviewer's reservation price.

As the saying goes, knowledge is power. It helps to get a glance at their cards before playing out your hand.

Ordinarily, the interviewer will volunteer a figure without too much prodding. But every once in a while you run into an interviewer who won't go first, despite your best efforts.

Like you, this interviewer has mastered the maddening habit of answering every question with a question.

YOU:	"What's your compensation plan?" (The suspense is killing me.)
INTERVIEWER:	"What sort of salary were you looking for?"
YOU:	"I'm open and negotiable." (The old standby.) "What would be a starting salary here for someone with my qualifications?"
INTERVIEWER:	"What do you think would be a fair salary?"

YOU: Well, I wouldn't want to be too far out of line with your overall salary structure. What kind of range have you allocated for this position? (*Please* tell me.)

INTERVIEWER: "What kind of range would you allocate?"

At this point your choices are to:

> Try and beat it out of him.
> Gracefully change strategy.

Usually, I recommend gracefully changing strategy.

You're going to have to make the first move. Hopefully, you've done some research into the position's probable salary range and have a rough idea of the employer's reservation price. Go at least 10 percent over this price.

Step Six (Assuming the Interviewer Has Just Made the Opening Bid): Go 20 Percent over Their Offer

After the interviewer makes his offer, let there be a few seconds of silence. This indicates you're thinking about it but are not too thrilled. Then go 20 percent over his figure, perhaps mentioning a qualification or two that supports your counteroffer.

Example: You are offered $30,000 as a fresh-out-of-school attorney. You pause, then respond, "Truthfully I was hoping for something more in the neighborhood of the mid- to upper-30s. I feel that my years of watching *Perry Mason* have given me a sound understanding of courtroom procedure and that this deserves some compensation."

The interviewer's opening figure is rarely his reservation price, no matter how sincere he looks. Undoubtedly he's given himself at least a 10 percent leeway.

In the above example, you estimate his true reservation price is closer to $33,000. Your counteroffer of mid- to upper- 30s is deliberately pegged just a little too high. It will allow you to split the difference and end up with a figure very close to his reservation price.

Naturally, you should let him assume (hopefully incorrectly) that the final settlement is very close to *your* reservation price and that he has been a skillful negotiator.

Sometimes there are problems.

Problem #1

Interviewer's opening bid is ridiculously low.

Temptation: Start talking about all the needy children you support; punch the interviewer out.

Recommended Action: Show your surprise and calmly go 10 percent over what you estimated to be his real reservation price.

Problem #2

Interviewer's opening bid is ridiculously high.

Temptation: Jump up and down with joy; kiss the interviewer.

Recommended Action (depends on how nervy you feel):

- VERY NERVY: Go 20 percent higher.
- Nervy: Go 10 percent higher.
- chicken: Say "I don't think we're too far off, but I would like a chance to think it over."

Whatever you do, treat the interviewer's figure nonchalantly. Conceal your pleasure.

Problem #3

Interviewer's opening bid is a range.

Temptation: Look confused ("They never told me to expect a range!"); start talking in French.

Recommended Action: Only pay attention to the top figure in the range and then proceed normally.

Problem #4

Interviewer won't move (either at all or far enough) from his opening bid.

Temptation: Take off your shoe and start banging the desk.

Recommended Action: Try to negotiate for:

- A bonus or an earlier-than-normal salary review, that is, rewards that are commensurate with performance.
- A broader position, that is, rewards that are commensurate with tasks and responsibilities.
- A different interviewer.

Perhaps I should mention that not *all* salaries are negotiable. Of course in the absence of reliable information to the contrary, it's always better to first assume the salary is negotiable and later find out it isn't, than vice versa.

There's really nothing to lose and everything to gain. The interviewer won't be put off. If anything, he'll be impressed by your spunk.

If it turns out the salary is nonnegotiable, politely ask the rationale behind this policy. Assuming the policy sounds reasonable and the salary is above your reservation price, don't push it.

Step Seven: Check Out the Entire Package

Fringe benefits are more than just the appetizer and dessert; they may account for a significant portion of the meal.

We're talking here about your basic add-ons, such as vacations, holidays, and insurance, as well as more exotic fare, such as moving expenses, company cars, and bonuses.

When comparing different compensation offers, make sure to consider the entire package, not just the salary.

Example: You have two offers. The first only pays $99,500 but includes your own private helicopter. This will save you $3 a day in bus fare, or $750 a year. Naturally, then, you prefer this offer to the second, which pays $100,000 but includes no such fringe.

Step Eight: Sleep on It

It's been a long day. You've tossed around a few salary figures and checked out the benefits package. Time now to go home, put on your pajamas, and mull it over. Don't make any hasty decisions while you're still in the same room.

It's especially important to play for time if you're still far apart on salary. A few days may allow the employer to readjust his budget and come up with a bit more money.

But even if you're perfectly satisfied with the entire package as is, it's still nice to wait a day and make sure you're not suffering from temporary insanity.

So get a good night's rest.

10
On Your Way Out

"Visits always give pleasure—if not the arrival, then the departure."

Portuguese proverb

Leaving an interview is like leaving your house. There are a couple of last minute things that need to be done, like turning off the oven and locking the door.

In another way, though, it's just the opposite since the idea is to keep the door open and the oven warm.

Before leaving, take a reading on where you stand. "Mr. Interviewer," you might ask, "how do my qualifications compare with what you're looking for?"

The interviewer could say:

1. "What qualifications? Your candidacy is a joke. I can't believe you had the gall to apply for this position."
        OR
2. "In my twenty years of interviewing, I've never met a more qualified candidate or a finer human being."

Both of these responses are good since they let you know exactly where you stand. Too bad you'll never hear either. Much more common is:

3. "Well truthfully, we're really looking for someone with

81

five years of experience, and you have only four years,
11 months so I'm just not sure."

4. "Your qualifications seem just fine."

In some ways, I'd rather hear #3. I figure the interviewer
has to have at least a *few* concerns. Voicing these concerns
allows me the opportunity to sway him over.

Hearing #4, I might probe further: "Mr. Interviewer, I'm
glad you find my qualifications suitable, because I'm very confident about my ability to take on this position too. I wonder,
however, if you have any unanswered questions or reservations
that I might address."

Remember, only the unspoken concern is problematic.

Also, before leaving, find out about their timetable. Ask
"Where are you in your decision-making process?" and then get
permission to call back at the end.

The goal is to take matters into your own hands as much as
possible. Avoid passively waiting for the phone call that never
comes.

There is often the temptation to leave the interview with a
dramatic gesture. You might, for example, bellow, *"I shall re-
turn!"* and do a triple somersault out the door.

Usually though, a simple "Thank you for your time" will
suffice.

After the Interview

11
Follow-Up
Tact(ics)

"The number of meetings, not the length of meetings is the key. . . . You send me a letter and a resume: we have met. You call on me for an interview: we have met again. . . . . In the emotional area, there are no clocks."

Eli Djeddah[1]

I told my dentist about this book. He pointed out that in some ways an interview *is* like going to the dentist.

"Take you and me for instance," he said. "I'm your only dentist but to me you're just another mouth. You'll remember me much better than I'll remember you."

It's much the same with the interviewer. He may interview ten to twenty people and after a while the names and faces will all start running together. In fact, he's more likely to remember the pastrami sandwich he ate last Thursday than you.

Your one advantage over the pastrami sandwich, though, is that you can send a thank-you note. The pastrami sandwich can only send indigestion.

The interviewer receives your thank-you note. His first reaction may be to burp. "What did I eat last Thursday," he wonders, "and who is this person sending me a thank-you note?"

1. *Moving Up* (Berkeley, Calif.: Ten Speed Press, 1978).

85

So he digs out your resume and tries to reconstruct what your interview was like. Your "message" has just been repeated. Advertisers understand the principle of repetition well—too well. When was the last time you ever saw a commercial aired just once? Probably never, or if you did you can't remember it.

In fact there's a whole literature about the optimal number of advertising exposures. Some suggest that at least three exposures is optimal. In a job campaign, this might translate as:

First Exposure: Resume and letter.
Second Exposure: Preliminary interview.
Third Exposure: Thank-you note.

The idea is to keep your name in front of the interviewer. The third exposure might just make the crucial difference in getting to the next round of interviews.

Strategic considerations aside, sending a thank-you note is also just plain courteous—plus it only takes five minutes.

Usually the very act of sending the note is more important than what the note says. If you like buzzwords, though, consider the "AEC" format:

A = Appreciate   E = Enthusiastic   C = Confident

For example:

Dear President Nixon,

I appreciate the time we spent together discussing the position of Supervisor, Watergate Break-In. I remain very enthusiastic about the position and am confident that I can make a useful contribution.

Your obedient servant,
G. Gordon Liddy

P. S. Am sending, under separate cover, what used to be my right arm. This is just my little way of saying "I'm with you."

A follow-up note can also be a useful place to restate your case or clean up any mishaps.

> Dear Mr. President,
>
> Remember when you asked me what my strongest qualification was to be Vice President and I went totally blank for ten minutes?
> Well, I finally remembered. It's my ability to think quickly under pressure.
>
> Yours truly,
Gerald Ford
>
> P.S. Betty says to tell you that I once spilled coffee all over her new suit too. Your joke about forgiving my clumsiness if I would pardon the cover-up still has me in stitches.

Other follow-up tactics include:

1. Sending a revised resume, specifically targeted to the position.
2. Sending a one-page summary of your career accomplishments.
3. Sending a one-page summary of "as seen by others," using excerpts from references of former employers and associates.
4. Sending a short paper expressing your thoughts on a subject of mutual concern.

Riskier ploys include:

5. Mailing a full-size poster of yourself.
6. Having your mother call up and give a reference.
7. Dropping a "Sicilian hint," for example, sending your

resume with a dead fish wrapped inside to communicate "hire me or you sleep with the fishes."

Follow-up is important, but getting the interviewer's attention isn't everything. He might conclude "If the guy is this weird *now*, what will will he be like *after* I hire him?"

12
When the Sky Is Falling

"Life is a tragedy when seen in close-up, but a comedy in long-shot."

Charles Chaplin

"Tragedy is if I cut my finger. Comedy is if I walk into an open sewer and die."

Mel Brooks

The worst part about rejection is that the Universe doesn't seem to care. I don't think it organizes its day around your career.

On the other hand, the Universe doesn't hold it against you either. So don't hold it against yourself. Avoid thinking "If only I'd done it right, things would have worked out." You just don't have that much control over things.

Rejection is usually nothing personal.

Actually, the odds were never in your favor. Suppose there were ten people interviewed. That means your chances were only one out of ten. Well maybe a *little* higher; after all, you did read this book.

The good news is that the more interviews you have, the better the odds. It's like betting on a roulette wheel. Odds are slim that your number will come up in any one spin, but eventually over many spins it will come up.

For example, the probability is better than fifty-fifty that you'll get at least one job offer after seven interviews (with seven different organizations), assuming your chances are one out of ten in any given interview. The proof of this is explained in the footnote below, but feel free to wait outside.[1]

For those of you who didn't go in, take my word for it; probability theory is the Universe's way of saying "cheer up."

Career consultant Tom Jackson has an interesting view of this. He sees interviewing as a process of collecting Nos on your way to the eventual Yes. His scheme looks like this:[2]

No, No, No, No, No, No, No,
No, No, No, No, No, No, No,
Yes!

The *only* way to reach Yes is by navigating through a series of Nos. Therefore, every time you get rejected, he suggests looking on the positive side: that's one more No out of the way before the Yes.

Consider, for example, the life and career of this man:[3]

Age 22:   Failed in business.
Age 23:   Ran for legislature and lost.
Age 24:   Failed in business again.
Age 25:   Was elected to legislature
Age 26:   Endured the death of the woman he loved.
Age 27:   Suffered a nervous breakdown.
Age 29:   Was defeated for Speaker.
Age 34:   Was defeated for Congress.
Age 37:   Was elected to Congress.

1. Proof: Let $.9$ = the assumed probability of not getting any given job (an arbitrary assumption).
Then $.9^7 = .48$ = probability of seven straight rejections.
$1 - .9^7 = .52$ = probability of at least one job offer in seven tries.

2. Tom Jackson, *Guerilla Tactics in the Job Market* (New York: Bantam Books, 1978), p. 118.

3. James Higgins, *Human Relations Concepts and Skills* (New York: Random House, 1982), p. 116.

Age 39: Was defeated for Congress.
Age 46: Was defeated for Senate.
Age 47: Was defeated for Vice President.
Age 49: Was defeated for Senate.
Age 51: Was elected President.

The man was Abraham Lincoln.

Or, for a more recent example, consider roughly a *year* in the life of Lee Iacocca:[4]

- He was fired at age 53, after working at same company for 32 years.
- His boss explained the firing by saying "Sometimes you just don't like somebody."
- He was deserted by close friends, including his best friend who never even called.
- He started to drink heavily.
- He developed the shakes.
- He considered suicide.
- His best job offer was from a company on the verge of bankruptcy.
- He accepted the job; he was later widely criticized and attacked for the company's worsening problems by the press, the U.S. Congress, and most business leaders.
- He was forced to give up his entire salary due to the company's rapidly deteriorating condition.
- He began waking up in the middle of the night, fearful of going insane.
- He started seeing double.
- His wife became sick with a fatal illness.

Five years later, Iacocca was acclaimed a hero, responsible for saving Chrysler Corporation and 600,000 jobs. The lesson of the story according to Iacocca? "Perseverance."[5]

4. Lee Iacocca with William Novak, *Iacocca: An Autobiography* (New York: Bantam, 1984).
5. *Newsweek,* October 8, 1984, p. 70.

But don't start celebrating right away. Let yourself be upset for a while if that's what you're feeling.

It's quite natural to feel disappointed, hurt, angry, or just generally bad. And feelings don't like getting pushed around or ignored. They need to have their say. There's nothing wrong with crying, pounding a pillow, or any other emotional release.

Now is the time to be nice to yourself. Buy yourself a present or do something you especially enjoy. And if you really feel bad, take a few days off before you go back to the rigors of job hunting.

Just because they rejected you, there's no reason to reject yourself.

"How can I use this?" is a question that Laura Huxley[6] suggests we ask ourselves when dealing with negative events.

For example, if you were a Watergate burglar and had just gotten caught, the question How can I use this? might suggest writing a prison novel.

The idea is to turn the tables on life, to recognize our power to be more than just passive and helpless victims.

The negative events can be large or small. A job rejection is a nice-size misfortune since it falls somewhere in between:

- Minor irritations, (sinus congestion or a stalled car).
- Major catastrophes (house burned down or nuclear war about to break out).

Here are some possible ways to use a job rejection.

1. *Get feedback.* Call up the interviewer and ask:
   a. How the hiring decision was made. The interviewer's answer may set your mind at ease: "I felt intimidated by your height, so I ended up hiring a dwarf."
   b. How you might improve the effectiveness of your campaign, for instance, your resume or interview

6. Laura Huxley, *You Are Not the Target* (New York: Farrar, Straus & Giroux, 1963), p. 70.

92

style. The interviewer might have some useful input: "When was the last time you changed your socks?"

Not easy to ask for feedback but often worth the risk.

2. *Ask for referrals.* Tell the interviewer that you remain enthusiastic about this type of position and wonder if he could recommend other people to meet with to explore similar opportunities, either inside or outside the organization.

He might say, "Why don't you call so-and-so, he's taller than a telephone pole, and he never changes his socks either." Or he might just agree to keep you in mind should he hear of anything.

3. *Maintain the contact.* If you sense some rapport with the interviewer (in other words, he didn't spit on you), stay in touch. You have just developed a new contact.

Consider pursuing the next immediate opening in this organization, even if you have taken another job in the interim. Do this by letting them know periodically of your continued interest.

Strangely enough, you may have a big edge over the next round's competition, just by virtue of being known. And if worse comes to worst, you'll get rejected again, which would provide an interesting challenge to the How can I use this? question.

4. *Revamp strategy.* When *was* the last time you changed your socks? Or took a hard look at any of the pieces of your job strategy, from resume to follow-up techniques? Now may be a good time to do a laundry.

Job rejections aren't easy. But consider this: What do the following things have in common?

a. Dinosaurs
b. The plague
c. Spiro Agnew
d. Your job rejection

Answer: They're all a bit annoying but only in the short run. In the long run we eventually feel better and even see humor in the situation. And in the very long run, we're all dead.

Sometimes it helps to take the long view.

13
Look Ma,
a Job Offer

"I guess it just proves that in America anyone can be President."

Gerald Ford, on becoming President

When I was ten years old I had to make an interesting decision: which of three summer camps to go to. I chose the one that showed a picture of people eating pancakes for breakfast. I liked pancakes.

The joke, of course, is that every camp in the galaxy serves pancakes; it's just that the other two didn't happen to mention it.

This illustrates one method of decision making; call it the Pancake Method.

Ten-year-old boys aren't the only ones who make decisions this way. The interviewer himself may have used just this sort of approach. Perhaps he offered you the job because you reminded him of a bowl of cornflakes. Who knows?

Some people take a dim view of the Pancake Method. Descartes, for example, would be one. Descartes, you may recall, is the philosopher who said, "I think, therefore I am." He could have said, "I eat pancakes, therefore I am," but he didn't.

Descartes would take a more rational approach to decision making, including the decision about that job you've just been offered.

Descartes might suggest listing the criteria that are important to you in a job and then evaluating the given opportunity against these criteria. Here are some possible criteria:

Day-to-day tasks and responsibilities.
Percent of time spent working with people versus data versus things.
People environment, especially boss and co-workers.
Autonomy.
Compensation; future earning potential.
Opportunities for growth and development.
Risks in the job, organization, and industry.
Pace; time demands.
Size of organization.
Organizational purpose, values, and culture.
Location.
Working conditions; office.
Amount of travel.

You've got to say this about Descartes: the man's systematic.

Hopefully by the end of your job campaign you'll have two or three offers to choose from.

Let's suppose it comes down to the following alternatives: U.S. astronaut or Mafia hit man.

The box on the next page shows how you might proceed. Please review it before reading further.

Although the hit man does well on categories like "Not tied to a desk" and "Work with people," the astronaut scores substantially higher on "Secure future" and therefore would be the preferred alternative.

Sometimes it's not this simple. Job offers, like pancakes, often don't come off the griddle at the same time.

Suppose you find yourself in the following dilemma: the Mafia has extended a firm offer (perhaps too firm), but the Space Program is still up in the air. What actions do you take?

Dealing with the Space Program is relatively straightforward. Don't pressure or give them an ultimatum. Let them know

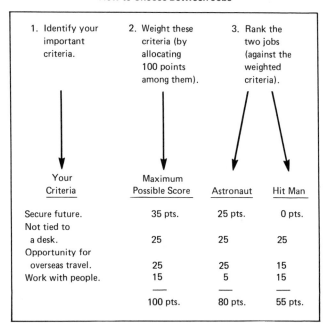

How to Choose Between Jobs

1. Identify your important criteria.	2. Weight these criteria (by allocating 100 points among them).	3. Rank the two jobs (against the weighted criteria).	
Your Criteria	Maximum Possible Score	Astronaut	Hit Man
Secure future.	35 pts.	25 pts.	0 pts.
Not tied to a desk.	25	25	25
Opportunity for overseas travel.	25	25	15
Work with people.	15	5	15
	100 pts.	80 pts.	55 pts.

that they are your first choice and ask if they could possibly take your time problem into consideration.

Dealing with the Mafia is trickier. You can:

1. At the very least, ask for a week or two to consider their offer. "Mr. Godfather," you might say, "this is an important decision for me. I intend to make a serious and long-term commitment, and I would be doing both of us a disservice if I made a premature decision." Whatever you do, don't let the Mafia know they are your second choice.

2. Decide whether you are willing to jump ship for the Space Program even after starting work with the Mafia—or perhaps before starting work but after accepting the offer, in which case it makes sense to negotiate a delay in starting time. (Actually, a four week delay in

starting time is good practice anyway—two weeks for notice and two weeks for vacation.)

Nobody can make these decisions for you but you.

Even if you're not dealing with the Mafia or struggling with different timetables, it still makes sense to take a few days before making a decision. At the very least, sleep on it.

Sometimes it helps to go back and ask some more questions. Try to meet with your predecessor or other employees with similar positions and backgrounds. Find out what it's really like working there, what people like and dislike about the organization and anything else that might be relevant to your decision.

This time, of course, you're in the driver's seat. It's like going on *The Dating Game* as the chooser:

- "Job #1, do you have any benefits that I might find especially desirable?"

97

- "Are you the kind of job that's going to demand my attention seven days a week?"

Just make sure your questions aren't too bizarre:

- "Would you get excited if I came to work one day without any underwear?"

In the end, there's still something to be said for the Pancake Method. In fact some people argue that this method isn't about pancakes at all but about listening to our gut feelings.

If rational deliberation gets you nowhere, try the following:

1. Flip a coin. Heads you take a given job, tails you don't. Live with the outcome for a while and see how it makes you feel.
2. Before putting your money away, ask yourself the million-dollar question: If you had a million dollars and never had to work again, would you take this job? Count yourself lucky if your answer's yes.
3. Consider a first cousin of that question: If you couldn't tell family and friends about the job, would that change your decision? Get straight on whether you're taking this job for yourself or to satisfy parental expectations, impress others, and so forth.

So much for pancakes. By the way, in case you were wondering, I had a pretty good summer at camp.

Epilogue:
One for the Road

"The universe is so vast and complex that if we needed books like this to become enlightened, we'd never make it."

Thaddeus Golas[1]

"From the moment I picked your book up until I laid it down I was convulsed with laughter. Someday I intend reading it."

Groucho Marx (on S. J. Perelman's first book)

If you ever write a book, don't show it to my dentist. Here's what he said after reading this one: "Anyone who reads this book will end up knowing more about interviews than you do."

I bared my teeth in annoyance, but he pretended not to notice. "The point is," he continued, "that they'll have the benefit of both your experience *and* theirs."

Sometimes my dentist is a real pain, but in a way he's right. Books like this can go only so far. From that point on, your own experience, not mine, becomes the real teacher. Perhaps you'll come back to these pages for a visit from time to time, but basically you're on your own.

Take good care of yourself.

1. *The Lazy Man's Guide to Enlightment* (New York: Bantam Books, 1980).

Appendix A:
A Word About
References

"Whenever a friend succeeds, a little something in me dies."

Gore Vidal

References are critical in a job campaign. Yet they are frequently handled ineffectively. Believe it or not, even your *friends* may be a tad ambivalent about giving you a rave review. And rave reviews are what you're after because in today's legal climate it's exceedingly rare for anyone to say anything blatantly negative about someone else. Faint praise, however, is a lot more common, and potentially deadly.

The solution is to choose your references carefully and then to provide them with ample information and treat them with courtesy. More specifically:

1. Contact your references at the very outset of your campaign. Explain your situation and let them know that you'll alert them before anyone actually calls.
2. Make sure to call each time they are likely to be contacted. Brief them on the position, particularly what the interviewer is really looking for. Remember back in the interview when you slipped into the role of detective

and asked specifically about this? (If not, review Chapter 6.) If the interviewer is looking for someone with good interpersonal skills, for example, make sure at least one of your references will stress this.

3. List your references in order of strength. The interviewer may call only one or two people, and he'll undoubtedly start from the top. Your last boss should probably be high on the list.

4. After you've found a job, send all of your references a written note thanking them for their help.

5. Avoid listing ex-lovers, total strangers, or Gore Vidal.

Appendix B:
If You've Ever
Been Fired[1]

Leo (July 23–August 22)—Your ability to laugh at adversity will be a blessing because you've got a day coming you wouldn't believe. As a matter of fact, if you can laugh at what happens to you today, you've got a sick sense of humor.

Andrew Rooney[2]

On Self-Worth

- No, there's nothing wrong with you. Nor is there anything wrong with having the thought "There must be something wrong with me." Just don't dwell on it.
- Realize you're in good company. Many of the most successful people in America have been fired. Review Lee Iacocca's story in Chapter 12.
- Review and practice at least several of the stress-reduction techniques in Chapter 5.
- Keep active and busy. Establish a daily routine and stick to it.

1. Special thanks to the outplacement counselors who advised on this section, particularly Dick Jandl and Steve Ford.

2. *And More by Andy Rooney* (New York: Atheneum, 1982).

How to Explain the Termination at an Interview

- Be brief. The more explaining you do, the more suspicions you are likely to arouse. Here's an example of a complete explanation: "About six months ago I got a new boss and our management styles were completely different." Period.
- If you must elaborate, imply that you're good but the situation stopped being appropriate. Talk about the merger, or the reorganization, or how the job just didn't evolve as hoped for: "I wanted to do all these things that turned out to be beyond the scope of the position."
- If you mention a personality conflict or difference in chemistry, make sure to add: "However, a lot of people in the organization are eager to serve as references."
- Don't bad mouth the organization or your ex-boss, even if the interviewer baits you by saying what a negative reputation they have.
- Don't lie. If the organization didn't go through a cutback or a reorganization, don't say it did. On the other hand, never use the word fired.
- Role-play your answer in front of a friend or a tape recorder. Practice until you're absolutely confident.

How to Explain a Long Period of Subsequent Unemployment

- Shorten it by including the two to four months you were receiving severance pay (if you were) as part of your employment with the organization. Just be sure to O.K. this with your ex-employer so that everyone's story is the same.

- Talk about how selective you are. Say "I've had some interesting opportunities" (if you have), "but this move is so important that I've made up my mind to do a really thorough search and hold out for the right position."
- Don't say you've been consulting unless you really have been for a good portion of the time and can actually name names and say what you did.
- Project quiet self-confidence. Don't act desperate, for example, by calling up every other day to find out about the decision.

What to Do About References

- Go back and see your ex-boss at the earliest opportunity. No matter how painful, this is critical. Act conciliatory and friendly. Your overriding goal is to neutralize him as a potential enemy.
- Show him your resume and share your career plans. Then pose this question: "What will you say if someone calls for a reference and asks why I'm not working here?" Odds are your ex-boss already feels terribly guilty and will not w 'nt to hurt you further. With you sitting in front of him, he 'll say the most positive thing possible and then *feel locked into this answer,* as if he made a verbal promise.
- If you're still uneasy, but it seems appropriate to list him as a reference anyway (for instance, he was your last boss, and not just for a three-month period), then alert the interviewer that this may not be the best possible recommendation: "I can tell you now that you're apt to hear about personal chemistry and our differences in management style." Do this in a neutral tone, without sounding bitter. This effectively discredits the reference and frequently deters the interviewer from calling at all.

Miscellaneous Advice

Finally, keep in mind some advice that the philosopher Nietzsche once gave regarding adversity: "What does not destroy me, makes me strong."

Try to forget the fact that Nietzsche is now dead.

Index

109